Columbus in the New World

selected poems

Dale Boyer

Artwork Credits:

Columbus in the New World. Artwork by Dan Holder, after Gericault, *Portraits of the
Insane* (collection of the author)

New Testament: Photo of the author's family by Bill Boyer

After. Demolition of the Paradise Theater, *Moline Daily Dispatch* archives

Print ISBN: 978-0-99701-346-7
eBook ISBN: 978-0-99701-347-4

Contents

For Scot,
my safe harbor

Columbus
in the New World

(1994)

Colombus in the New World - Contents

"Mother, Father, listen: I was not born but made."

Mark Doty, *Art Lessons*

I.

The Long Voyage Out

Looking at the Moon Inside the Aerospace Museum

Ambling alone through darkened corridors, backlit
among the bright disasters of the cosmos:
nebulae, star-clusters, distant suns,
I am remembering July the 20th, 1969,
my father calling through the dark across the lawns,
"Dale. Day-el. Come inside now. This is history
you're missing."

                It was a moonshot
he was asking me to be a part of, even though
at that point I was feeling other pulls,
already warping from his orbit —
father looking at me strangely
as I walked into the summer-humid house:
"What were you two boys doing down there?"
"Nothing. Me and Stevie Kurtz
were playing with each other"—
blushing as I thought about the timid exploration of
our young boy bodies in the moonlight. Even then
my father's and my words were separating, phrases
jettisoning context like a rocket ship its early stages.
"Well, you come in here and watch this, now —
I want you to remember."

                Truth to tell,

I can remember little now but static,
rocky surfaces and endless tests: Neil Armstrong
dangling one foot above the moon, encapsulated
and suspended there while waiting for the word.

I've been a disappointment to my father.

Though he never told me this, what words are necessary
for the dropped ball, the averted eyes, the father
soon not even tossing to the son?
It was an image I was looking for — an image
all that senior summer when I pierced my ear —
those long, red-haired and angry years until
I finally brought Rodney home.
At what point did the moon, wrenched from the
earth's side,
find an orbit of its own? At what point
did the waters of the wound at last become pacific?

It's history I'm missing. Father,
back there in your blue remove,
must our worlds stay so parallel?
Can't anything be done?

                    Now as I stand before
an ashen photo of the moon, its surface
rendered with an icy clarity, another father and his son
begin to make their way about this artificial semi-dusk,

the father taking time to introduce the boy
to all the wonders of the universe. Dad,
let me make some introductions of my own:
I am your big bang. I'm the cell
divided many times against itself, the universe
exploded and expanded in your wife, into the back wall
of the uterus, into the emptiness outside it.
Can't we find some neutral ground, some language
of forgiveness and respect? Give me some sign —
just one small step?

Beside me now, this father hoists the child
up to his chest, points at the moon, and says,
"Mira, la luna." It's a way of introduction.
It's like saying, "Father, this is Rodney.
Rodney, Father."

Dad, the words mean: "Look, the moon."

What Can You Say?

A word is spoken at the dinner table. It's a word
that once connoted happiness. But now,
it stuns your mother like a stone. It halts
utensils full of peas and stuffing
midway to the mouth. It silences
ensuing holidays.

Two lovers roll from one another
into empty spaces. Lips
that fumbled over body parts
now seek to utter words. A newspaper
out in the intersection
tumbles over
lazy as a cat. The window
hums in sympathy
with passing trucks.

The jangle in the penis fades.
The penis shrivels up into itself.
The sun comes up each morning
in a slightly different place.

The Response

It is not so much my mother
slamming doors and hurling biblical quotations
from the top of stairs who troubles me,
although admittedly —
that is, more than I'd like to say — she does;
it is instead my father, turning wordlessly away,
who, as he draws the door behind him,
turns a last time,
showing me a face that says
not so much, "You have disappointed me," as
"I wish I were not alive." All this
resulting from a word I brought to them
as gently as an egg upon a spoon, a word
I'd carried with me all my life, though jammed down
deep inside my pocket like a ticket stub.
I once wrote in a poem,
more from agenda than the heart, I think, that
Poetry is the art of erasing connections.
I know now that's not true: it is the art of finding them
in places you did not know they existed. Father:
were you thinking of the time you held me
naked to your chest, a moment
I've remembered all my life
as one of absolute, unparalleled affection?
Mother: did you realize it didn't come from you?

An egg is cold and profitless unless some warmth
attends to it. Left standing there between the two of you,
a choice between two doors, two different paths,
what other choice was there except to follow
what my heart dictated? Mom; Dad: given half a choice,
I would have followed you.

Phase

I. "Dad," I said, "I'm gay."

"Yeah, well, congratulations.
Just don't ever bring your boyfriend home."

This is the place where you'd expect to find support,
redemption. Was I wrong to put it right up front?

II. Things change. The blue-grey ice cube
with its steel aurora

floats
as it diminishes.

III. Propensities, proclivities: these are the heart's
disease.

Proximities, propinquities: these are its sad
iniquities.

IV. Ease, ease, I say.

V. Mom's dead. Dad's
gone now, too.

(This is the place where all the tension ought to be. Isn't it sadly unaffecting at the end)?

VI. *God damn you. Please.*
These are my black doxologies.

*

Epilogue: [insert an image like the ice cube,
that redeems and dazzles,

here].

My Father Meets My Lover

Once I cared about my name. It was a seed
I wanted planted

in the furrow of another.
Now I know it's just a movement

of the tongue,
a shaping of the wind,

not so much spoken as
released.

Homer Loses the Thread

My father is the worst storyteller I've ever heard. You'll have to take my word on this. He can lose you like a pair of glasses, set you down somewhere and not know where he left you. I can't do it like he does, the way he stops to reach for words that float about elusive as a dandelion seed; the way he gets sidetracked on unrelated things; the way a sailor might if, starting out upon a journey, tall ship bobbing visibly down in the harbor at the street's end, he remembered that he needed extra thread for mending sail and, setting off to find some, met an old friend who convinced him they should have a drink together. At the pub, the two men might remember an old flame and, feeling love rekindled, set off suddenly to find her. Along the way, the two might disagree about who'd loved her more and, fighting finally a duel to settle it forever, kill each other on some barren field. You understand the drift? The thread is never bought, the ship abandoned. Love is never found, and our tale runs aground lamentably astray, unseconded, obscure.

Some things are just irreparably lost: things like the way the raindrops sounded on the tin roof of the trailer that my dad built out of scraps, the trailer we took all of our vacations in when I was still a child. The sound was sharp, distinct, and loud, yet strangely comforting. It rumbled like a load of acorns pelting on a car roof, but it had a softer sound than that. Inside the trailer, it was warmer than the outside, so the ceiling clouded up with condensation, which we kids would write our names in. You could feel the tin charge running through your bones, like biting down on foil.

It was probably a sight, that trailer. Dad was quite a saver and a bargain hunter. He'd buy lots of things at one store by the name of Railroad Salvage, which was just exactly that: a store that dealt in damaged goods from train wrecks. I remember eating lots of dented canned goods as a boy, and drying off with towels from various hotels, with names like *The Ambassador*, or *Park Place Manor* stitched in red across the middle. He'd go on and on about the deals he'd found there, all the money he had saved. He could bore you stiff with all the details. Finally, you simply had to walk away.

Now, stepping from my lover's shower stall, I think about my dad, about how hard it was for him accepting I was gay. "I have to say, it's sad to think my genes will end with you," he said to me one day. We're almost out of soap, and I make a mental note to jot it down. I grab a thick mauve towel to dry myself and notice that it's raveled slightly on the end. I grasp the loose thread at the base, and try to break it with no pull. What was I thinking? Oh, yes, soap. And trying to concentrate on that, I snap the long thread off and drop it softly in the trash.

I Am the Apple of My Father's I

After a hot bath, my balls distend themselves
away from me. Perhaps I shouldn't write

this, but it's something
that my body does — I can't control it.

It's nature's way of making sure
the sperm are safe, the temperature consistent;

it's the apple falling from the tree and rolling slowly
outward through the parched grass: seeds.

Now as I stand here in the garden
thumbing large black peppercorns deep into earth,

I think about my father's sole advice to me:
"Son," he said, "never put a thing in writing."

Preparing for Departure

On Tuesday afternoon,
I pull up to the airport's weeded edge
and sit there, watching.

I've imagined my farewell so many times.

The planes line up,
then slowly lift away. Hour after hour,

they line up and
they go...

The Bodies on the Lawn

I used to love small towns, but now they're dead
to me. As snow falls,
it speaks only of obliteration.

Mother, father, there are just two
types of parents: those who let their children be adults,
and those who don't.

You see I had no choice.

The bodies on the lawn are sheeted now with
snow; I heed its white command.

I've had to kill whole towns.

II.

Columbus in the New World

His first, imprecise love convinced him forever that the beloved object must dwell in the distance, and I believe this conviction sealed his fate as a lover. During the next days he went back to every corner ...to reconstruct a landscape of memory. He thus laid out a Casale of his own passion, transforming alleys, fountains, squares into the River of Inclination, the Lake of Indifference, or the Sea of Hostility: he made the wounded city into the land of his personal unsated Tenderness, an island (presage even then) of his solitude.

Umberto Eco, *The Island of the Day Before*

Columbus in the New World

Even on his last trip through the islands,
lost, withdrawn, it was the same:
each time his prow split sand, Columbus raced up
like some poor, dim duck, imprinting
on the startled group of Arawaks assembled
by the glass green waters of the sea,
demanding of the men excitedly,
"Where is the Khan?"

Columbus in the Plague Years

How the natives welcome him!
And how magnificent they are, decked out
with egret feathers, turquoise beads
and necklaces of bone;
they flash broad, yellow teeth
and welcome him into the fold.
He loves their greased black hair,
the strong, young limbs, the loincloths
hanging dirtily about the midriffs of the men.
A musky smell enfolds them like an aphrodisiac.
He passes through the crowd ecstatically, admiring them,
and pauses here or there to kiss a handsome face
or chest, or nudge a leather loincloth back.
He does not notice as he touches nipples
lovingly, or runs his tongue along the hairless limbs,
the gullies of the backs, or down
into the dark ravines of buttocks,
that the tribe is dying all around him. Waves of them are
falling to the ground, dogs barking frantically.
There on the shores of this New World,
he sees the village flattening like wheat.

A Trip Across the Border

Skulking through the plant-draped atrium
inside the Sheraton, Toronto,

skirting past the lazily mobbed ballroom
hosting the trade show I'm supposed to be attending,

dodging eyes and walking swiftly down
the saw-toothed escalator, I move quickly

down into the underground of this fair city.
Past the housewares laid out temptingly

inside The Bay, into the subway where I check the stand,
but do not find what I am looking for,

on into Eaton Centre with its latticed glass and steel dome
overhead, and still not what I want; into the light

across the street from the restored Pantages
Theatre where *Phantom of the Opera*

enacts its nightly drama (ugly man
in love with someone beautiful); on down the garbage-

scattered street, the dirty red and yellow neon
circling endlessly and pointlessly; still one more block

to Edward street, I turn at last
and creep into a store called BMV. Inside,

on faded blue-grey carpeting, beside the racks
of battered paperbacks which no one really comes for –

only here do I find what I want, squeezed in between
the plastic-wrapped tri-packs of *Penthouse* magazines

and porno movies: *Strength and Health*, *Physique* and
Muscular Development, but in back issues

from the early 70s and 80s: Mike Mentzer,
Kalman Szkalak and a hundred others, flexing

20-year-old muscles, radiant with health: Pat Neve,
posed against a Bicentennial flag, the zenith of
male physical

perfection. I remember many of these issues, snuck
these magazines
into my home and worshipped wide-eyed at these altars.

I remember when the world felt young
and beautiful.

Desire

Desire is a racecar
hurtling down the track
in flames.

In the debris, they find
your body,
charred and fetal,

in the trunk.

Northern Exposure

This town collects lost souls, its residents washed up along the granite stones of an Alaskan riverbank like fish spawn, owl down, eagle feathers bluish-grey and white. Look at the odd assortment:

Joel, the displaced Jew from New York; his some-time girlfriend, Maggie: young, Amelia Earhart type who's run away from Grosse Point; Chris: philosopher and D.J., recently released from prison, who is more or less the whole town's voice of consciousness. They're all here: astronauts and Eskimo, half-breeds and 60s refugees, even two gay men who run a bed and breakfast at the edge of town. Somehow, they all fit in.

That's how these hit shows are — that sense of effort-less community. That's why I find myself so often tuning in: "Sometimes you want to go where everybody knows your name; and they're always glad you came." This is the town

a lone moose stumbles through each Monday eve-ning, lost, relationless, and sad. I hope you know this place, because I'd really like you just to be here with me for a while as we tune in, watch the moose pass by the *tromp l'oeil* paint-ing of the palm trees on the tropic isle, and ponder it, con-fused. The people here collect in one place, mostly: in the town's one diner. In one episode, the diner closes, and the people don't know what to do. Joel fasts and tries to find a vision, to become an honorary Eskimo. The cafe owner, in his 60s, tries to find a star up in the sky that he once named for love. They all are

trying to find their way, the way I did when I first came here to Chicago, visiting the bars to meet somebody, counterfeiting faith on Sunday mornings at the MCC, or agitating actively for AZT: I was a gay man looking for a niche in his community. Still hoping

to be made an Eskimo, Joel asks his friend, "What does belonging to a tribe mean to you, Ed?" His friend says, "Bingo."

Weeds

(in memoriam)

The gorgeous blooms went first, plucked
like irises
by children's hands from gardens. After all,

what butterfly was able to resist
a flutter in those holes, set so alluringly
there in the middle of those downy plains —

what rugby-shirted bumblebee a drag
among those bright, sweet, sticky fluids?
O you busy bees, at work there still,

refrain: see how the huge, pink-headed peonies begin
to rot, their faces pressed for too long
in the mud? See how

the other flowers die untimely,
everyone is wearing black,
and weeds have taken over?

Now, I stand here in this dark bar in my charcoal suit,
a dandelion stuck in my lapel:
Death, pass me by.

A Sunday in the Early Fall

You walk the streets among the gathering debris,
the detritus of summer underfoot.
It crackles brittlely with every step.

The neighbors in the house next door are readying
for fall: the blue steps leading down
into the drained white swimming pool. Their daughter,
Emily, starts preschool in a few days. Nick,
their son, will be attending kindergarten.

In the slow, inexorable diminution of the year,
you see your breath before you like chastisement:
it is all you have produced. Now, standing

at the edge of summer's playing field,
you see that last night's rains
have washed the chalk-marked lines away.
A solitary dog runs unattended to its furthest edge.

At home again, you sit and watch the football game
on tv, looking up from time to time
as though expecting that a child might toddle in the room.

Your friends know what they're doing with their lives.

Saturday Night Fever, 1991

Exiting the rental store, I step out quickly,
head bent forward, studiously looking at the ground.
The video is tucked beneath my arm, as if
it were an ordinary rental, something
that I wouldn't be ashamed to show to friends.
The slightest interaction is a risk:
—"How are you?"
—"Fine. And you?"
—"Just fine. What movie did you rent?"

To stave off this scenario, I try to think of
recent films to answer with, and yet I meet no one.

I meet no one, and try to block the memory of
the man back in that room
who kept on looking at me as I moved among the aisles,
trying to avoid his gaze; to pick a movie quickly
from the wall of gorgeous nudes. I was afraid
to look at him, and when I did,
his eyes fled like a startled doe's.
What kind of men are we, trapped in the
sad synecdoche of porn? What were we doing there—
there in that sleazy place, both with the same needs,
staying well away from one another?
Yet, the video is safer. It's a sure thing.

These days, you can never be too safe.

*

Now, as I watch, bathed in the blue glow
of the television screen, two naked men
begin to touch. My hand roves restlessly
in counterfeit of that; a shameful rag is near.
The one man takes the other
by the shoulders, turns him over,
and — quite ostentatiously — puts on a condom.
Everyone is properly protected.

This is how gay men make love.

Columbus at the Bijou

I want to rise up
from my faded velvet seat
here in the darkened theater

where they are showing, more or less
continuously, *Powertool*,
Rear Admiral, and *Sailor in the Wild* —

rise from
this lazy equidistance of old men
bathed in the flickerings of flesh —

rise up and muster courage
for the walk up toward the EXIT sign
beside the screen,

pass through the door
and mount the black steel spiral staircase
to the second floor. I want to move then

down the brown-tiled corridor
made slippery by wads of cum,
walk past black-curtained cubicles,

each with its separate glory hole
drilled through to the adjacent box
where married men and scared teenagers

rid themselves of urges
they can't carry back into their lives.
I want to pull the curtains down,

I want to look into their eyes.
I want to lead the way
into a braver world.

The Origin of Consciousness in the Breakdown

There's something wrong with him. See how he lingers,
rain-soaked, on the empty el platforms:
he really has nowhere to go.

Out in the bay,
a dolphin that's escaped from the aquarium,
still leaps up expectantly each day
at 10, 12, 2, and 4.

"Tribeless, lawless, heartless one."

There's something wrong with him: he's lost the murmur
of whatever god once spoke,
and now, blind bard, spouts garbled text
and exploits of a hero long since gone.

Homeric homo homeless *sans* Patroclus.
("He had fallen in love with the past: a profitless love.")

Look at him, all huddled in the doorway,
staring at that window,
hoping for the light to flicker on.
In rain,
a cat yowls on the stoop.
Somebody, let him in.

Tarzan as a Gay Man

Think about it: living on the fringes
of society,

the cry that echoes
tree-to-tree, impinging on

the native ear, exhorting
nature in its unfamiliar ways — a cry

that makes the whole world shrink in fear.
Who is this man — Tarzan,

Fauve homme sans tendresse,
part of Africa, yet not a part. Nobody wants to think about

his urges, what's inside his heart,
its surges. Mark the way he spends his days:

he swings from emptiness-to-emptiness,
just him alone (Jane was a phase).

Remind yourself he's swift and strong. Say it again:
he's fearless.

The Man in Walgreens

Standing there as gorgeous as a man can be —
the man I'd seen so many mornings on the train —
dressed up in business suits and starched white shirts,
now wearing crumpled tennis shorts, a sweaty Harvard
t-shirt,
stopping off to buy a few last-minute things
at 9:00 one humid summer evening; glancing for
a moment
at a *Harper's* on the newsstand; un-self-consciously
attractive; trim and handsome, with that sort of
gentleness and elegance about him that was
so heartbreaking;
I, disconsolately walking through the aisles until
I spotted him, attempting to remember whether there
was anything
I was forgetting; trying not to look too obvious
as I concluded quickly I was done, then moving up
behind him
in the line; he standing there in front of me
a little to the side (he was afraid he smelled bad,
I could tell, but somehow this considerateness made him
even more attractive); swinging absent-mindedly
the basket
with his goods. And, as he placed them on the counter top,
my mind engaged in various scenarios of introduction

as I watched him prove his bachelorhood: milk (just one
quart); orange juice (again, a little skinny quart);
6 eggs; a loaf of light rye bread; and lastly,
crushingly, the Tampax for his girlfriend. Maybe
there is nothing so unusual in this — perhaps you'd call it
just another case of someone who is unavailable.
To me, it is the essence of America.

Winter, Chicago, 1985

I was like a person
waiting for an elevator to arrive:
the button pushed, the rise and fall
of currents in the shaft, the strangers
gathering, directional, near me, but still
the doors not opening.

That year, I found a haunt
inside the strange cleft of a bridge
beneath an overpass – a spot
where drivers slowed on seeing me,
glanced anxiously around,
then waved me in.

In Africa that same year: drought.
So famished were the villagers
that when, at last,
supplies arrived for crops,
the people ate the seeds.

III.

New World Views

We have it in our power to begin the world again.

Thomas Paine

At the Therapist's

In the consultation room, the light subaqueous,
the dry hum of the heater sounding far off in the distance,
I am silent, subcutaneous,
when suddenly my therapist walks in and says,
"Oh my, it's dark in here!" and flicks the dimmer high.
The room is flooded with a warm, bright light —
who'd turned it down?—
and now my spirit starts expanding like a sponge.

—Just like the tank I once saw at the Shedd Aquarium:
huge, lumbrous catfish, tawny brown and black;
bright, striped angel fish that must have been two
feet across.
The sign on the display said: "Common North American
tank fish will grow to fit whatever space they're in."

Archaeology

It is one thing
as one walks about the excavated city of Pompeii,
to conjure up the flight along the broken cobblestones,
fire raining down on shattered plinth and pediment;
the last, black breaths of cinder air
as people huddled on the beaches, fearful,
trying to secure a boat out on the roiling sea —
one thing to view the antique, golden, snake's-
head bracelet
with its ruby eyes,
and try imagining the arm that once slipped through it;

it is something else again
to wander through the ruined landscape of one's own life
and attempt to do the same: to comb the earth
like tourists on the field at Gettysburg —
to try to rescue some stray fragment from the dust
that indicates precisely where the battle turned,
or how the fight raged on.

A poem is a dead thing.

Reappraisal of a Sunset, San Francisco

Sunset, the reddish-orange glow
among the sawdust California hills,
and I am sitting once again across from you
in Madison, midwinter, barlight glinting amber
in your glass of Guinness Stout,
and you, gold California boy, are telling me
you can't believe how short our sunsets are.
Perched on this hill above the bay
these long years later, I can see now what you meant:
the languorous and multi-hued gradations
of the light, the slow, protracted interplay
of tones above the ocean, daylight dulling into
butter, amber, rust, then fading
even softer into ochre and carnelian—
I can see the length and depth of it, and know.

Back then, though, in the fleeting light of January,
in the midst of grad school poverty,
I didn't have a clue, did not know
how to answer your seductions — only sat there
so intensely hard and scared that, later,
when I finally stumbled drunk from you
to take a pee, I had to wait five minutes
till my dick died down.

Where are the beautiful gay love scenes?
Where are the bright examples where a man
slips in another man as gently as the sun
into the sea?

Rick, after we had climbed the creaking stairs
to your apartment, stood there in the frigid darkness
for that awkward moment while you fished for keys,
our breathing visible, my gonads small as acorns,
I was still not certain what was going to happen —
if I even wanted something to. But then
the door was opening and you were pulling me
inside the dark, moist room to smells of cat food,
rotting garbage, washcloths slowly souring,
and I was feeling suddenly your clumsy tongue
deep in my mouth, the vise grip of your hand
upon my penis, and the bristle of your beard
against my lips. I smelled the ashy odor
on your clothes and hair, mixed with the acrid,
almost overpowering scent of perspiration
as you rubbed me up against your prick,
your two hands clamped upon my buttocks,
prying hard, as though to tear me wide. Disgust,
desire and nausea engulfing me, I let your tongue
move down the soft slope of my mouth, then lift
and suck the oyster of my tongue
as if to rip it out.

For years
I could not leave that room, could not
get over hating you, and yet I understand at last that
rarely has complicity been more confusingly arrayed.
It took a gentler hand, a little kinder lead,
a closer and more honest look into that night. Rick,
it has taken every second of my 30 years
to get me here, to see this light myself,
to get past thinking that, in winter, sometimes,
in the Midwest, half an hour is all that's necessary
for the world to slip from daylight into darkness.

What I Did With My Allowance

Pumping up the hill to the Convenience Mart
at 12th and 41st streets in Moline,
my bottlefly green Stingray sleek beneath me
with its black banana seat
(sharp yellow racing stripe straight down the center),
I was breathless as I winged out past the grade school,
blacktop listless in the summer sun,
rode into the intersection at 12th Avenue,
then turned to ride past blistering tennis courts
beside the junior high where I'd just finished seventh grade.

How shall I tell you this? At 13,
on a lazy summer day,
school out and all the courts deserted,
I was off to buy a muscle magazine.

I'm not sure what your attitude toward this
will be — a lot depends. I only know that
as I raced to the Convenience Mart that day,
my body weak with lust, excitement, fear,
my pockets jingling with change, already
I knew I was doing something wrong.

Nobody else had ever had the thoughts

I had — none of my friends or family,
with whom I'd go each Saturday
to Sundstrand's Market; there,
beside bananas resting on their artificial turf,
I'd sneak a peek at *Strength and Health*
or *Muscular Development* — chance one scared look
at huge, bronzed men who flexed their monstrous arms
on palm-lined California shores while women
(and a small boy) gazed in adoration.

Nor was this the only time
I ogled these physiques of power:
beneath my bed I had a stash of *Popular Mechanics*,
comic books, and other magazines
with ads that made my groin melt:
"Be a He-Man! Gain 10 pounds of muscle
in a week! Add inches to your chest and arms!
Slap pounds of virile manhood on your frame!"
I never had the least desire to take
this course myself: that is, I wanted not
to conquer love, but have love conquer me.

At what point does desire become perversion?
At what point does the mind accept the verdict
that one's longings are perverse?

In junior high, I had a friend named Ted.
Ted was athletic, handsome, all boy. That's
the quickest way to state it. I regret that
that's the quickest way to state it. Ted was blond,
tall, wiry. I had known him all through grade school;
now, in junior high, I started noticing
the way his hair looked as it framed his face,
the way he looked in clothes, the muscles swelling
in his chest and arms. In gym class, I would dress
beside him at the lockers noticing
the bush that had begun to sprout between
his legs, the small hairs on his ass and upper lip,
the snaky line of growth down from his belly button.
He'd stride confidently naked to the showers,
his penis — long, thick — bouncing heavily
against his sallow skin. I saw it in the other boys
as well, especially athletic ones —
who sported moustaches or hair on chests,
while I was still as scrawny as plucked chicken.
Swimming with my friends those summers at the Y,
I noticed surreptitiously the way the Speedos outlined
buns and penises, looked on in awe and longing at
the straining muscles of the men who worked out
in the weight room of the gym,
snuck into bathroom stalls in sad attempts
to grapple with my shame. The year my youth group
took a trip to Canada — eight Lutheran sophomores

bouncing in a van on backwoods Minnesota roads —
Ted's head fell gently into slumber on my shoulder
and I left it there, until a jouncing motion
woke him up, and he, as startled as I was,
did not discuss it.

*.

Here is what I did with my allowance:
I did not tell the other boys in gym,
"Your bodies are all marvels. May I touch them?"
—Did not tell Ted, "Your head fell on my shoulder.
It felt wonderful: the warm silk of your hair,
the pink flush of your cheek. I am attracted to you.
Might you be attracted to me, too?"
In high school, when the other kids were pairing off
and dating, I would take the car and sneak away
to Readmore Bookworld in Rock Island,
(small, squat cinder block perched on the one-way
outside town), stand frail and scared at lunch
among the horny businessmen absorbed
in *Oui* and *Cherry*; growing nearly faint with longing
as I stared at bulging biceps, chiseled abs —
at muscles blown so huge
I stood almost an hour at a time, so paralyzed
by fear, so stiff with lust, that I endured
the gruff shoves of the straight men walking past
to dwell among such godlike company.

I was 23 before I kissed a man.
It took me ten more years
of running home from senior proms
and dances that I didn't want to go to, masturbating
furiously to my precious, hidden video of *Pumping Iron*;
ten years of therapy and loneliness
and running into friends down at the mall
with wives and kids and no idea that I was gay;
of reading Personals and having drinks at sleazy bars;
ten years
of forays out into the city's vast, carnelian night —
of walking upstream through the currents of
religion, self-hate, fear, the condemnation of
society, the disappointment of my parents
'till at last I felt the firm hand of a man
smooth out the twisted wreckage of my soul
as certain as a sculptor.

I have strayed indeed.

Here is what I did with my allowance:
After pumping up the hill to the Convenience Mart,
enduring all the agonies of picking out
a bodybuilding magazine, its hulking specimens
displayed so prominently on the covers,
I took my money to the counter, gingerly laid down
the naughty publication, counted out the change

half-faint, and heard the clerk say, "Man,
what you want this for? These are for faggots."
Peddling home, upset, ashamed, the magazine curled
awkwardly around my Y-shaped handlebars, I real-
ized now
there was nowhere I could hide. I rode long distances
in order not to meet with any friends,
could not go home, I thought,
since I was far past sin, far past
the sheer perversity of anyone I knew,
and wound up, strangely, on my grade school playground
where, after I'd looked at some few pages
of these men with bodies like the gods, I took
the magazine and buried it — this emblem of my difference —
as far down in the dumpster as I could.

The Other Room

For Scot

We'd been kissing on the couch,
and for the first time ever, everything felt right.
For years,

I had been tethered to the dock,
a small boat, banging madly
with each passing wave.

"Why don't we take this
somewhere else?" I said
impulsively. My statement

startled me as much as you.
But, when our eyes met,
it was like a sailor finally coming into port.

We walked together, nervous, to the other room, and
through the open windows, I could hear
the soft plash of a fountain

in the plaza far below. Your bed
was pushed against the wall of windows:
soft-lit city in the evening.

As you led me to the bed, I thought:
Here is a guy whose headboard is
the sky.

Portolan

Your face across the room
was like
the ending of a journey:
fading spray, the cry of gulls,
a glimpse — perhaps —
of land. Love!

Something heavy
drops from me, straight
to the bottom, bursts
into the warm sand,
holds there with its hook,
then all is still.

Sails slacken
as the hull rests
on the mythic shore.

Geology, Construction, Time

Once I helped my father add onto our house:
between the two of us, the walls rose neatly,
evenly, each 2x4 in place, the long rectangles
marking out the space where soon a family
room would be. The leaves fell through the roof,
the walls were open to the wind, the sun spilled
down on us: he in his white v-necked t-shirt,
tall, long-side burned, thin, a cigarette
or line of nails tucked in his lips. Me:
just a boy of 8 or 9, bone thin, bespectacled already.
With his ropy limbs burned red by sunlight
as he moved through match stick walls, he was a god:
his hammer came down thunderously on the nailheads;
he consumed huge mounds of food at mealtimes.
As I stood beside him in the bathroom sometimes
when we peed, his dick seemed unimaginably large.
One day, on coming to the final corner of the room,
I said, "What happens if the sides don't meet?"
imagining a gapped seam like a flattened box,
the walls bowed out to let in wind and rain and light.
"Don't *meet*," my father said, as if amazed.
"Well, hell, they're going to meet — you don't think
I'd be that far off now, do you? They may be
a little off from square, but we can cheat some.
When we nail the joists in place they'll come around."

Dad, some things never do: the earth sometimes shifts up
and heaves. Try as I might to build a home
like yours, I couldn't build a thing more solid than
anxiety, my penis drooping like a bent nail
at the door between a woman's thighs. And so
I left behind your world of picket fences, drifted
into cities where there were no houses, no foundations
I could build upon, and came to rest at last
here in the arms of one who understands my pain —
a man who shores me up, who'll help me carpenter
whatever thing it is we're building with each other.
Even now, he has his arm around me, here,
in full view of these families on vacation,
though the action takes me by surprise.
He's telling me, I think, we have a right,
we're just like any other couple, things
have got to *change*. I feel uncomfortable with this
but don't step from the link, I guess, because I know now
nothing ends up where it starts: some houses
tumble finally into the sea; some ocean floors
get thrust into the sky. The mountains here in Canada
were once the coastline of a continent near Ecuador.
Dad, do you see where I'm going?

Columbus With the Aged Gays

I was born aught five, my dear. In Cuba.
Cuba, Illinois, that is — gotcha!
That makes me eighty-eight, Columbus Day.
I've been to Europe over thirty times,
taught Shakespeare all my life. I graduated
Harvard, class of 1933.
I have a letter from Virginia Woolf;
can't find the damn thing anywhere. I still swim
every day; get up at four. Have to.
We get in there before the swim team does.
You circumcised? I'm not. I see these young bucks
standing in the showers, and I kid them that
they're missing
something. They're not certain what to say.
You certainly are a beautiful boy.

                              Of course
I never dared come out: society
would kick you in the teeth if you said *gay*.
You hid it deep if you were in the service.
I was stationed over there near China.
Helped them build the Burma Road. The Army
even gave us all male bearers, Asians;
made a pass or two at mine: no luck.
My God, I'd love to kiss you.

Saw Noel Coward hooted off the stage.
You know Noel Coward? Praise be. Was chatting up
a lifeguard at the pool the other day —
a gorgeous thing, but straight — who'd never heard
of Oscar Wilde. Clueless! It gels the mind.
Well, Coward, of course, was gay, sophisticated,
and urbane, and here he is performing
for a crowd of lusty, butch GIs
who haven't seen a woman in six months.
Got off the stage just barely with his life;
hopped off the edge and landed in my arms.
He was as shocked as I was, I can tell you.

I have never had a lover, never. Sad.
Had sex a bit, but it was pretty sordid,
dropping to my knees in back rooms and the like.
Fact is, I'm 'retro-gay.' I was sixty-four
when Stonewall happened, sixty-four. It was
another decade 'till I got the balls
to damn all the torpedoes, man the hatches
(please excuse my puns) and come out big.
Nobody in my family ever knew; few friends.

You kids have got the world in front of you —
the world: make sure you take it. Hold my hand
a moment, would you darling? You're an angel.
You're a sight for sore eyes. You're a dream.

Linnaeus at the End

"A series of strokes muddled his marvelous memory.
A pupil recalled seeing him 'be led down into the garden,'
and remarked of the man who handled and defined more
kinds of plants than any man of his time that he 'delights in
the plants but no longer knows them.'"

-Joseph Kastner, *A Species of Eternity*

He fondles dandelion, cattail, milkweed pod,
and does not think: *class, genus, species.*
He does not even think *weed, herb, or wildflower,*
nor resort to Latin. He cannot recall
the sexual system he devised for all of them,
nor why a pistil or a stamen need determine anything.
He merely rises in the hour of chicory,
and has a distant memory of mornings
filled with softnesses like this: a downy memory of color
rising and emerging from a fog, the lake;
the soft blue hue of summer mornings,
milk blue light upon the pillow;
of a cheek as soft as morning glories
in the dew. He walks among the plants
and does not judge them. Do you understand?
He smells the sweet rot of the ferny floor,

where fiddle heads are poking up among the leaves,
moves out into the vistas of the New World,
blank, and emulates the bumblebee,
which lights on anything that shines.

Stonewall 25th Anniversary

Some trees need a fire
to start their seedlings; redwoods

germinate this way. Centuries from now,
they'll tower proudly here.

May those who find them bring a flame.

New Testament
(Revised Standard Version)

2006

And so we must go back again, and start from the beginning to find out what the holy is. As for me, I will never give up until I know.

Plato, *Euthyphro*

Erasmus says that every serious student must read the entire corpus of the classics and make his own notes on them.

Anthony Grafton, *The New Yorker*, 2007.

Contents

Genesis

The spirit searcheth for all things, yea, the deep things of God.

I Corinthians 14:10

The Apple

At lunchtime, reading my *King James*
the way one reads *The Golden Bough*,
a slice of red delicious
hits the page.

I've always been dismayed
that *knowledge* is the source of
Eve and Adam's banishment —
that understanding represents unpardonable sin.

Oh, I think, distressed to see
how deep the stain has penetrated
to the other tissue pages:

Now I'll have to get a different book.

The Mysteries

On the blacktop at the school one day,
first grade, or maybe second,
I remember sliding down the metal pole I'd climbed —
a basketball hoop on a field of
hopscotch squares, the kids at recess.
As I slid, I felt the adolescent version of
orgasm: sharp, metallic somehow.
I had never felt a thing this startling or intense, and
I tried tirelessly to duplicate it:
sliding down the banisters, the basketball poles,
down the tripod metal legs of slides and swing sets.
I could only recreate it sometimes,
and it wasn't ever quite as vivid as the first.

In grade school, I had kissed girls,
felt the squishy insubstantiality of their lips and limbs,
but I preferred the muscles of the boys,
the hard shells of their chests.

                        In junior high,
I spent an overnight with Chad Smith —
muscular, athletic boy – and, in the night,
he climbed in bed beside me.
I knew right away this was transgressive; I knew
I should want the bodies of the girls,
so soft and ineffectual.

But,
as I felt Chad's body near me — felt
the hardness of his young boy limbs,
the firm, warm, tender motion of his muscles —
it was like a long slide down a pole
straight into something else.

The Museum of Religious Artifacts

In the Topkapi palace in Istanbul
the rooms contain
illuminated manuscripts,

crosses, Korans, menorahs…
Increasingly, the objects grow more dubious:
St. John's cooking pot,

The Mantle of Muhammad,
The Staff of Moses.
As I walk, I think:

Some of these objects may be real, and yet,
I find it difficult to believe…

Theogony

I saw a man once in the locker room
down at the Moline 'Y.' Stripped naked,

striding to the scales, he was a glimpse of
heaven: massive chest, a warrior's limbs,

and hair that curled along his body
like an exhaled breath. It frothed and furled about

a penis thick with powers of engenderment;
his balls were silk-swathed eggs.

To my astonished, adolescent eyes, the man was God.
As God flexed all his muscles in the gym,

I jerked off in the dark beneath the stairs.

Exodus

"Come!" [The word may also be translated as "Go!"]

Note to Revelation 6, *Oxford Annotated Bible, Revised Standard Version*

Lavender

In sixth grade,
at my mom and dad's insistence,
I tried out for basketball.

I had never played the game before —
at least, not in any organized way —
that is, enough to know the rules, or even

concepts like offence and defense. We practiced
one or two nights in the gym,
then played our first game at McKinley — old,

dark, brick school in an unfamiliar part of town. There,
in the last five minutes of the game,
the coach ran up to me and said,

"Take number 16. He's your man."
I didn't have the slightest notion what he meant.
My teacher seemed to sense this, then said,

"You know, stick with him. Cover him."
I can't recall now if I found the right boy or,
if, when I found him, what I did; I just recall

the searching and the awkwardness,
the sense of not being sure exactly
what I could or couldn't do with hands.

Something else I still remember from that grade:
three words
for which there are, apparently, no rhymes:
orange, silver, purple.

The Intersection

Once, in college (small-town Illinois)
I walked the country roads behind the school.
Love seemed unattainable; I loved a boy —
a love, at that time, I could not admit.
The pastures spread away bucolically;
cows gently grazed the bundled hay.
A gravel roadway intersected mine,
and as I stood there, indecisively,
a guy from English Lit. jogged down the hill,
shirtless, providing me a little thrill.
He had a body that could make one drool;
he neared; (I guessed he'd pass me by, then split).
But Wade stopped suddenly in front of me
and leaned down, huffing, chest hair whorled
'round nipples sweatily. I didn't know Wade well,
but he intrigued me: this was '83
and I was still quite naïve sexually.
I'd sometimes wondered if Wade might be bi -
(I'd heard from others he was often high,
and this adventuresomeness in the tame Midwest
fueled dreams about those arms — that chest!).

We stood beside the softly mooing cows
making our small talk as he drew his breath;
I still can see Wade there beside the fence,

reciprocally scared (I now know), tense.
My heart beat wows and little deaths, mind racing
with the sudden possibilities. We both were
facing some big fear, uncertainties
whose terrifying end meant we were queer.
He went his way, and I went mine,
the need unspoken: fruits left on the vine.

Still to this day, that memory's a goad;
In some ways I have never left that road.

The Retreat

Lying here in bed propped on my elbow, nearly 45,
I am remembering my ninth grade church retreat:
mid-winter, Oregon (small town in northern Illinois,
but with the white snow covering the dark green
pine boughs
in that hilly and secluded Mississippi valley,
it could just as well have been in the Pacific Northwest).
I had a crush on Ron Wilcox, the church youth
leader: thick
brown mustache hanging sexily above his mouth,
his body small, compact and wiry. Lying in the guitar-
singing circle opposite him, cozy
in the January-heated cabin, I could see the bulge of
testicles and penis outlined in his jeans —
fixating on them as we sang in unison, "I am a rock;
I am an island," or, "We've only just begun."

                                    All
the other bright and happy teens, most of them paired
boy-girl,
boy-girl, and me there, shy and bookish, growing more
and more
aware of Ron as *male*: the way his thighs filled out
his jeans,
the way I caught a glimpse of underarm hair

as he played, the way the white shell necklace rested on
the black hair of his chest, the way his lips moved as he
sang, "Hail,
Jesus, he's the way, the way, the way."

Today, I saw the movie *Spider Man*, and for the first time
as I watched young Peter Parker flexing newly-hard-
ened muscles,
coping with the jism-webbing spurting from his wrists,
I understood at last the body as a vehicle, the way
the boys my age were fascinated by their powerful new
chassis;
why they sped off, dating, in their sleek machines,
while I lay masturbating, secretive, alone,
my body not so much an object of conveyance as
a road.

The Spin

In high school, feeling suddenly the pull
of boys, I made a friend of Andy: big,
strong kid who loved to work out. Once,
he locked me in his arms and spun me
'round and 'round.

                 Powerless
to free myself from the centripetal (or centrifugal?)
force, but also from the overwhelming feeling of
his muscled pecs, I held on
breathlessly: that broad, hard
chest now suddenly
the center of my
world.

Chronicles I

There is no beast of the Apocalypse, only small terrified wantings.

Cal Bedient

The Way of All Flesh

Odd memory: in high school,
serious, withdrawn,
I read *The Way of All Flesh*.

It was not a class assignment. It was summer,
and our van was heading to the north woods
for a youth retreat up in the Boundary Waters.

Wind whipped though the van,
and we sang, "Carry on my wayward son;
there'll be peace when you are done."

Sunshine on boys' legs: hairy, summer-tanned.
The drowse of driving, and – for me alone – the heady pull
of sex.
As we drove on, I read while all my classmates dozed.

I don't remember much about the book
except one image: bees
that buzzed against wallpaper flowers,

sad, deceived. I had a crush on Matt –
well-hidden, though I snuck peeks at him as he slept
beside me. Later,

in my tent propped on the lake's edge
in the campsite we had reached by hiking and canoeing all
day long
(the only way into the region),

Mark, my tent mate, climbed on top of me and started
humping –
something I had heard he'd done to other boys,
but couldn't quite believe. I shoved him off, to know-
ing giggles

from the other tent. Mark was the boy who vaulted off the
nearby cliff
which everybody else was scared to jump from,
twenty feet down to the lake below; he came up fine.

With that, the rest of us plunged in as well.
A few years after college when I saw Mark,
he was obviously "out,"

while I, still living with my parents, was still as balled up as
a leech.
One last thing that I recall about that book:
the spine was badly cracked, exposing honeycombs
of glue;

each time I read a page, it fell away,
the volume dwindling to nothing
in my hands.

After the Party

A sudden, disapproving look out on the street, and
I'm remembering
the way I stared one evening during high school at Jim
Johnston's chest,
the thin white shirt stretched taut against his startlingly
adult frame;
an inch or two of hairy belly showing just above his
tight jeans
as he stretched out on the light beige shag. I looked down
from my perch above him in the La-Z-Boy, awestruck
to see the way the muscles bunched and swelled
beneath his perfect, 17-year-old, unblemished skin.
Only looking up did I see suddenly that
Jim was watching me watch him.

I looked away, but I'd been caught, and I can still recall
Jim's look, the shame that surged in me — the fear
that he would call me out. There, in the midst of
high school couples kissing, groping, drinking
in a basement rec. room in the Midwest, 1979,
the thought of being pegged a "fag"
was crippling. But, even more,
in Jim's eyes, I was recognizing

what I'd barely just acknowledged
to myself.

I left the party quickly then
to find my way back home
on unmarked roads
alone.

Joseph and the Dreamcoat

My college town, Thornton, still had a main square in the center, with red brick roads on all four sides, flanked by an Ace Hardware store, an IGA supermarket, The Farmer's and Merchant's National Bank, and a fine men's clothing store called Ricchiardi's.

One day, taking a break from class, I entered the store and found a beautiful green and pink striped shirt on a remainder rack for $14.95. Shocked that such a beautiful shirt was on sale for such a low price, I asked if there was something wrong with it.

"No," said the heavy-set, middle-aged clerk. "But, no man in town will apparently wear anything with the slightest trace of pink in it."

Scared to go against the grain myself, but also taken with the beauty of the shirt, I asked to try it on. The man looked at me a bit askance, and when I came out with it on, touched both my shoulders, taking in its measure. My groin stiffened immediately at his unaccustomed touch.

"There you go," he said. "Looks like it was made just for you."

Spanish

In college, I took Spanish: it just seemed the way to go.
I tried out phrases like: *La luz ya esta encendido* —

And told my hunky friend it meant
"The light is on." Then, looking in his eyes, I said,

"It kind of *really* means,
'The light's already on.'"

That was the dawn of coming out —
admitting to myself that I was gay.

Oh yes, I was a big old 'mo:
La luz ya esta encendido…

I Kings

If you bring forth what is within you, what you bring forth will save you. If you do not bring forth what is within you, what you do not bring forth will destroy you.

The Gospel of Thomas

In Gatsby's Closet

1979. I am working at the laundromat
in high school, washing clothes, dry-cleaning
while the other kids are at the dances or the football games;
behind the counter reading *Gatsby* weeknights, weekends;
moved by Daisy's breakdown in Jay's closet
as she touches all his unattainable silk shirts, his ties.

And, once a week, on Saturday,
near 2:00, the gorgeous, tall, athletic bachelor appears
with one week's worth of clothes
sprayed heavily with Jovan's Sex Appeal,
which I, attendant, take in willingly, wash
with that extra special care, folding
each sacred boxer brief and undergarment lovingly,

and hand him weekly back
without a single word.

Monologue Inside a Bar

I'm too much in my head. Tonight, for instance,
I was standing talking to a man:
good looking, waspy-thin, a baseball player type
with blond hair, wire rims. Told me that he was going
off to Yale divinity, and that intrigued me —
that contrast between the physical and spiritual.
High in a corner of the bar, a monitor was showing
bodybuilding tapes, and I was feeling drunk.
Of course, I wanted to go home with him, but thought
I had to make some conversation;
so we stood there talking for a while,
and then, before I know it, boom, this guy walks in,
short, stocky, not bad looking. Anyway,
he sidles next to him, this guy that I've been
talking to, and in a matter of about 5 minutes,
he's leaning over, whispering into his ear,
and in a blink the two of them are off,
not looking back at me still standing there
with one beer in my hand and in my head the bi-
furcated question, would you like another?
I was shocked, I tell you.

                    It's just like the time
a poet gave a reading at my school; I loved his work:
huge, vivid, warm. When he arrived,

he was the same way: mammoth, rumpled, sensual.
I spent the whole day talking poetry with him
and later found out he had slept with Becky Phelps,
a girl that I knew well — a pretty girl, I grant,
but one who must have thought synecdoche
was someplace in New York. She asked me, later,
if I had his books and I, imagining
that she was trying now to understand his work,
loaned them to her. I still remember how
she gave them back to me: bemused,
a little sheepish; how she turned to me
before she left and asked me earnestly,
"How do you pronounce his name?"

             I don't belong here anyway—
me, standing like some aging French professor
with my grey tweed coat and woolen scarf
among these beautiful but empty-headed youths.
Not that I teach yet, mind you, not full time,
and certainly not French. Sure,
I can read it decently, but that's a long way off
from speaking it. Just once I'd love to
launch into a totally spontaneous exchange
with someone, break outside my thoughts and fears
and live more boldly in the world,
the way this bodybuilder on the screen
plants both feet on the stage
and shows off his phenomenal physique.

Oh, how I'd love to fall
into the brute unthinking arms
of men who care about their bodies.

Reading *The Young Eagle: The Rise of Abraham Lincoln*

Nights, ensnared within his private civil war,
he works the late shift at the laundromat,

removing sloe gin fizz stains
from crinkled summer whites

of all the beautiful, night-clubbing men
with girlfriends on their arms,

their shirts unbuttoned to the waist, exposing
black-haired pectorals

and gold chains lying softly
on their collarbones;

he, with his plans beyond this little store,
this backwoods country village,

reading Thomas Paine, The Bible, Gordon Merrick.
"He was trying to put together

the fragmented pieces of his personality into
a coherent pattern;"

"almost without friends;"
"a long, gawky, ugly, shapeless, man."

Tennis Lessons

In my mind's eye all these long years since,
my seventh grade math teacher, Mr. Webber:
tennis coach; the man I saw each day in summer
with his shirt off on the courts:
dark clouds of dense black chest hair;
greeting me each day for lessons;
demonstrating how to grip the racquet with a handshake;
grabbing my hand with his hand,
the wood now at a 45 degree slant in between us.

How I wanted to dissolve into
the tablets of his pecs,
prostrate myself before the altar of
his thighs,
have him enfold me in those thickly swollen,
blue-veined biceps,
the scene repeated in my adolescent fantasies
so that he became (and is so, still)
a kind of practice board I'd pound myself against
each night, religiously.

God: he was the one.

Midwinter, Madison

In the small, local deli that year,
taking a break one Saturday while working on my Master's,
I still can see the tall, dark-haired, athletic-looking guy
in nerdy, Clark Kent glasses, svelte in a white v-necked
t-shirt,
his biceps straining at the seams –
clearly besotted with another man.

It was the first time I had ever seen a thing like this:
two men in love, in public, open. How I stared and stared
—

me at my stark Formica table near
the cloudy, much-erased blackboard with all its daily
"specials,"
painfully alone right by the door, hit with an icy blast
each time somebody new walked past.

Love Must be Reinvented

-Jean Cocteau

Maybe there's a reason why, inside the falsely day-bright
7-11 store
at 2 a.m. one Saturday, I stick the candy bar inside my
jacket pocket,
even though I have the money, never stole a thing before;
or why, this morning, soaping up inside my parent's avocado tub
while visiting them for my twenty-year reunion,
I begin to masturbate without compunction, furiously,
jism pearling on my hands, then washed in milky globules
down the drain.

Perhaps there is a reason for the loneliness of high school,
or the shock of finding out last night that Matt, a boy I had
a crush on
all those panicked, scared-stiff years ago, has died of AIDS:
the boy I followed to his Pentecostal church, enduring all
his talk of sin,
damnation; never telling him I was in love with him, but
keeping even to this day
the Bible he once gave me.

Maybe there's a reason for the moon and stars,

or for the idiotic grin with which the moon seems to be
mocking me,
but, as I climb into my car outside the store
I know there's not a reason in the world –
It isn't lighting up a Goddamned thing.

Chronicles II

God cradles us, only we can't feel it.

Jean Valentine

The K.A.P.O. Club

I.

When my Grandma died, nobody thought
to disconnect
the ice-cube maker.
We didn't think about it
sitting there, dysfunctional,
as all those cold half-moons kept forming
in the emptiness, eventually
filling up the dark and pushing,
pushing at the door, until at last
they spilled like carp
onto the fern-and-flower linoleum
of the kitchen floor.

II.

The way those little orange fish, inert
in hibernation, wriggle suddenly
up from the muddy bottom of the pond.

The way my mother, at the funeral —
both days — wore pink.

"It *is* spring, after all."

III.

A photograph: in childhood,
Mother in a garden, eyes cast down.

What's wrong with this?
This is the saddest picture I have ever seen.

Frozen here among white trellises
and fountains, lupins and hydrangeas —
in this children's garden
of enchanting flowers and innocence —

my mother looks ashamed.

IV.

It's the little details that get lost:
The way Grandma would never tell me
what her club's initials stood for —- K.A.P.O. —
she would take it to her grave; the way
she stood there in the hallway some nights
screaming at my drunk grandfather,
"Just because your wife's not interested
doesn't mean that you can't take it down the hallway."
Or the way Mom cowered in her bed
as Grandpa filled her doorway
once again.

V.

Some things come to light in time:
the iron pipe my Grandpa beat my mother tender with;
the queasy "maybes" at the back of Mom's
remembered touch.
 But others
stay as secret as the K.A.P.O. Club's initials.

Who knows what it means?

Abuse Poem, *a la* Gertrude Stein

(*For my mother, Donna Mae Erickson*)

You may not ever find the love you're looking for.
You may/will not ever find the love you're looking for.

You, Mae: never.

A Visit to the Grade School

When we were young, my brother, Larry, and I used to fly
our kite together
here above Ben Franklin Grade School.

It's a light-cream-brick affair that dates back to the early
1960s: sliding glass doors
on the classrooms, which look out across the fenced-in
blacktop, painted with

the yellow lines of hopscotch, four-square, basketball. Out
past the area
where we had gym and recess were the swing sets, monkey
bars, and baseball field.

Way at the farthest edge there was a gravel road, and then a
steep ravine
dividing Moline from the next town.

*

Am I taking too long setting all this up?
Forgive me - I am trying to fill some gaps.
In Pompeii, when they first began to excavate
the town, the archaeologists were puzzled at
the cavities they kept discovering

within the lava. Soon, somebody filled
a void with plaster, made a cast.
That's how they pulled out, one by one,
the forms of all the people buried in the stone.

*

I remember walking on these fields at Little League or
recess, playing kickball
on the blacktop, riding bikes up here with Larry in
the summers;

In the fall, we'd play together in the woods, dam up the
creek and watch it overflow,
or rake the leaves into a mini-mountain down in
our ravine,

then run and jump into the center, cleaving it with glee.
At Halloween,
we'd roam the neighborhood like burglars, black-masked,
going door-to-door with pillowcases

for our booty: we were going down the river with each
other. Oh, the days slid by as fast as slides slicked with wax
paper, which my mother doled out like a favor.

Then, in second grade, my brother flunked
while I went on to win a reading prize.

*

In math class in the seventh grade, my teacher
tried explaining "parallel" to us:
"Two lines, if they are truly parallel,
will run forever, side by side, not touching."
It was a concept everyone resisted.
"Won't the lines touch someday?" someone said, or
"Won't the lines just wrap around the earth
and then they'll cross?"

*

Perhaps it wasn't so much a question of parallel lines as
right angles.
Once, in Kindergarten on a play day, I remember putting
on a dress,
a mop-top wig and high heeled shoes. The teacher sent
me down
to see the principal. It is a walk I still remember:
down the green-tiled, strangely silent hallway,
past the classroom where my brother — failing, no doubt,
even then –
sat squirming in his first grade classroom;
past the other open doorways where the lessons rang out;
down the long, long hallway where I made my sharp
left turn
straight into ostracism.

In my older summers, I remember going to the
Bookmobile excitedly
on summer mornings,
while my brother and his stoner friends snuck *Playboys* in
the tree house
They'd start little fires in garbage cans, or pelt me
in the alleyway with acorns. They stole cigarettes as well,
and smoked them down in the ravine where once we'd
played together.

                              In college,
I came out and Larry moved out, working at a local
factory.
Too quickly, he acquired the weight of pre-ma-
ture, indentured
servitude: back bowed from holding up despair,
eyes narrowed to the width of objects rolling past
on a conveyor belt. In time, I might have passed him on
the street
unless he spoke my name. He grew obsessed with finding out
the names of his real parents (he was adopted — that was
Larry's cross),
and, in the course of tracking them down, lost himself. Now,
he has moved to California, and my parents don't know
his address.

Yet, on that March day I'm remembering, the two of us sat
here together
on this long, oiled telephone pole near the baseball dia-
mond, flying our kite —

the flimsy wood-and-paper thing we'd made together. It
soared above the school,
a red triangle tugging at the bowed end of a long, long,
string. We reeled it out excitedly

into the wind, into the blue sky and the clouds above the
deep ravine,
until at last the string snapped.

Fragments of a Lost Kite

Larry and I sitting on the heavy,
wooden, lime-green teeter-totters in the schoolyard;

me, suspended in the air – his prisoner –
and Larry asking me repeatedly:

"How much will you give me if I let you down?"

Puncture

Sitting together on the side of the tub
after our Saturday night bath,
Larry said, "Let me clean out your ears!"
So, taking the Q-tip,
he pushed it in and in:
at that age, who could know where other people's bound-
aries were?

I still can feel the orange-yellow pain —
can still remember all the dried-up blood and eardrops
afterwards, for weeks, and

Mother screaming,
"Look at what you've done to him!
You could have damaged him for life!"

And Larry hearing: "*Him,
our natural son; not you.*"
At that point, even I could hear
the difference.

And ever since that day, the void
just to my left
where Larry was.

Adopted Son

for my brother

Hatched from indifferent sand,
the green sea turtle plunges headlong
for the sea,

to swim his decades in an ocean
broken only by the distant songs of doting
whales.

Gardening and Its Associations

Rhubarb is my grandma Erickson,
floating giant lily pads
upon magenta stalks:
Its leaves are poison.

Violets are my mother:
simple, childlike,
trampled.

Flowering almonds are my Grandma Boyer:
delicate, old fashioned. Dad and I
stood in the yard one day, and he admitted finally,
"That bush is dying out."

Larry is the clump of weeds that's tossed away
and takes root
somewhere else.

My dad is carrots, which we harvested each fall,
hands frozen, raw. *They're so much work!
And I don't even like them that much!*

And me? I'm dandelions:
I survive.

Leviticus

I feel certain that if I could have been seduced by some gentle, understanding man when I was fifteen or sixteen, I would have avoided a lot of pain.

Henry Bauer, *Farm Boys*

Leap Year Winter

After all this time, I suddenly start echoing the party
line again:
"But two men loving one another —it's just *wrong*.
The Bible says so. And, our bodies aren't designed for it.
What am I thinking?"

In this sudden loss of nerve, I'm like a Catholic —
long lapsed — thinking to myself one day
with absolute conviction: *I am going to hell.*

Or like the revolutionary, after years of fighting,
setting down his gun before his friends and asking,
"What's so terrible about the government? Really?"

In this mood, I am moving through the bustle of the city:
sexless crowds of unemployed and homeless people,
bundled up and flapping aimlessly as pigeons
pecking at stray bits of broken glass. This is the populace

that has accepted its defeat, that knows that
Malcom X is dead. In February snow,
a black man's outstretched palm, the color of
a rained-on fire.

Horror Films

Back in the 70s
with Brad and Matt —
my constant high school friends —

we hung in Matt's new basement:
dark green velvet sofa,
stainless steel swag lamp and white walls,

watching HBO (a new thing).
They had just begun to show *The Omen*,
and one Saturday, with all the lights out,

we watched, riveted:
Matt in his tight white shorts and tan legs
on the sofa next to me,

blue tv glow accenting blond hair
on his legs; Brad: tall, athletic, on the other side,
placing me between them with my nascent demons.

I can still remember my desire mounting,
struggling against it like those Bible pages
pressed against the walls and windows in a vain attempt

to keep the devil out. At some point
when the hounds of hell were suddenly attacking,
Al — Matt's big black lab — decided to be bold.

He jumped up on sofa, terrorizing us as if he were
the spirit of the devil made incarnate. But,
it was not the dog that terrified me:

it was love.

*

In college — Spring break, 1983 —
I stayed on at the dorm with several other friends
who chose to work instead of going home.

We gathered in the darkened room with Jim,
a stocky, bearded boy
who lived just down the hall from me;

Tim: a soccer player, ropy-muscled, kind;
and Paul, a red-haired English major
I'd been hoping secretly was gay.

We turned the lights down low to watch *The Shining* –
Stanley Kubrick's horror movie
where the writer's trapped inside

a vacant, snowed-in ski resort.
It had a slow-build kind of menace;
and the line that creeped me out the most was

when the butler said,
"You've always lived here, sir," – meaning that
the writer had been stuck there all through time.

We watched, and secretly, I watched
the play of shadows on the chest and arms
of Paul and Jim and Tim. We laughed

and acted as if all the scares were minor.
Later, though, in walking down the empty hall alone
(no secret intimations any of them might be gay —

what else was new?), I felt a cumulative dread,
shrugged off a shiver, ducked into my death-still room
and locked the door. Turning round,

I started when I saw my own reflection,
looking back at me.

The Message

I was fairly certain that the group beside the gay
pride march
was not supportive; but, you never know:
some groups are out there saying, "God is love,
no matter what." And, their brochure was pink, so
I thought,
Maybe...

As they smiled and thrust the flyer in my hand,
I read the cover:
Does God want you to be proud of being gay?

A few steps later, opening it up, I saw the **NO!**
inside. I think I even chuckled to myself:
Of course not. What did I expect?
I wadded it and tossed it in the trash.

But now, my actions trouble me:
Why didn't I protest their message of abuse?
Why did I swallow it so passively?

Spring Break

Weeveling myself into you in the bed that night,
the cheaply paneled room with walnut floorboards,
badly scuffed,
blue satin blanket on your water bed — *sanctum sancto-
rum* —
I was sleeping with you finally, trying to tell myself
that it was normal: two friends bunking with each other;
burrowing into the warmth; kidding myself that
you as object of desire had disappeared — that it was just
the warmth and comfort I was moving into.

But then you sputtered into consciousness. I felt it:
your gaze fixed upon the other wall. You saying:
"Hey, bud."
"What?"
"Can you move over?"

And — incredible to me now as I think of it,
me throwing my arm over you in one last, desperate act to
maintain innocence
(or one last gamble?).

But again your stern admonishment: "Look what
you're doing."
"What?"

"You're trying to hide in me. You're acting like it's nothing
— like we're just friends.
But it's more than that.
It's sex."

And that word stinging like a slap: the first time
I had seen myself like that: clutched in a ball on one side of
the bed
and true love, self awareness: knowledge — facing me
upon the other.

Why are moths drawn toward the flame? Somebody
told me
it's an optical illusion —
that they're trying to move into
the even greater darkness
on the other side.

The Disease

I've been in love, and I've been loved. The first is better.
Katherine Hepburn

That summer I was sick and he was married now,
But still there was his dog to feed.
Why had I been left to care for him,
this creature huge with appetites
and so consumed with need?

I couldn't do it — couldn't stand up on my own,
my body swollen with its strange disease. How could I
walk the six blocks in this wavy heat to him?
I had to find somebody else: the man in white
who brought me medicine, somebody – anybody —
could you
take him off my hands for just one day?

And I did find a substitute. But, he came back in dreams:
he showed up at my door. He'd found out where I lived.
So, then I had to beg. I had to find new friends. I tried
pretending he belonged to someone else —
as though I never needed to go back.

But then, of course, I did. And when I did,
he was so happy that he peed on me,
and I just stood there, letting him.

On Staring Too Long at the Sun

Shirtless, the tall, lean boy next door
stands in the driveway
hosing down his red Camaro.
He's got faded blue-jean cutoffs on,
a beer-can in his hand, a single
golden stud in one tanned ear.
The radio is blasting out Metallica,
and after we've stood talking
for a while, he says at last,
"Yeah, you can help me if you want—
just don't fuck up the chrome."
He hands the hose to me, and I can feel
the water coursing through the rubber,
ebbing out onto the sudsy car
like freshly-popped champagne. It melts
along the rounded surfaces
in whorls, and I can smell
the wetness of the pavement,
the new black rubber wheels,
and hear the small thuds of the foamy water
sliding off the car. He crouches
near me, working up a lather
on the fenders, and I catch the fresh,
warm, oily scent that rises from his body.
I reach my hand into the bucket

for the washcloth, and his hand collides
with mine; he hardly seems to notice.

Later, when we've buffed the hard, red vessel
to a sheen, used Armor-all
to clean the leather of the seats and dashboard,
Windexed all the windows to the point where
they reflect the trees and sky,
the tall, lean boy next door says,
"Let's go cruise for chicks. This car looks hot."
And so I slide in from the other side,
he tossing down a towel hastily before I sit,
and feel him settle sweatily beside me
in his own uncovered seat, the scraggly
golden hair along his long legs
catching sunlight beautifully,
my own pale, black-haired thighs adhering
to the seats uncomfortably as we peruse
the teenage streets hormonally,
relentlessly, the t-top panels taken out
and summer wind caressing through his hair.

One day, the tall, lean boy next door comes home
with shoulders sore from pitching in a baseball game,
and says, "I guess I'd let you rub my back,"
and so I do, attempting not to look
too interested as I feel the muscles move

beneath my fingertips, then slide my hands
down to the sharp declivity of spine
and start to work the area above his ass.
He lets me do this for a while; then,
when I move my hand a bit, leans back and socks me
on the jaw. The blow stings like a 2 X 4.
I do not move and he does not. Then,
pointedly, he looks away, and I move back
to where I was.

                    One fruitless Friday night
the tall, lean boy next door comes back
and says, "I guess I'd let you suck my cock,
but try to kiss me and I'll pound you." So I
kneel there at his feet obediently,
trying not to anger him, to keep my throat
as wide as possible, my teeth out of the way,
because this moment
in a basement here in mid-America
is all I've ever dreamed.

Footnote King James

"To what extent we, too, are still pious." Nietzsche

Unstable as water,
I am a brother to dragons, and a companion to owls.
My skin is black upon me, and my bones are burned with
heat. [1]

Behold, the Lord passed by, and a great and strong wind
rent the mountains, and brake in pieces the rocks before the
Lord; but the Lord was not in the wind: and after the wind
an earthquake; but the Lord was not in the earthquake: And
after the earthquake a fire; but the Lord was not in the fire:
and after the fire, a still small voice. [2]

I am like a pelican of the wilderness; I am like an owl of the
desert. [3]

---

[1]   The last word of the Old Testament is "curse."

[2]   Anxiety has no place in the life of the faithful.

[3]   The words may mean "There is no God and I am exhausted," or
      "I have no God, yet I endure."

Leviticus 20:13

Blue-black threat of storms;
A strange, unearthly calm.

When at last we touch, it's like the snow alighting
on a bough.

Ruth

There are, it may be, so many kinds of voices in the world, and none of them is without signification.

1 Corinthians 14:10

Jan Morris and the Meaning of Nowhere

(Jan Morris lived and wrote as James Morris until she completed a change of
sexual role in 1972).

Exile is no more than absence, and it can take many forms.

His national origins were indeterminate. His manner
was a mixture of the florid, the stiff
and the deliberately outrageous.

He had explored
the homosexual stews of Karachi, and investigated the
polygamy of the Mormons.
He did not solve the mystery.
Organically inclined towards neurosis, he himself found
only failure:
Night after night I see him peeling off his gloves with a
sigh to return to his lonely lodgings. *Goodnight, Herr
Doktor. Better luck next time, eh?*
Here is another cameo of exile's disillusionment:
Bound together only, whether willingly or unwillingly, by
the imperial discipline,
head held high, emerging from a pile of Roman ruins,
*I was the world in which I walked, and what I saw
or heard or felt came not but from myself.*
A great quarrying gash in its flank ...suggests to me a scar
of surgery.

The officers have turned in their saddles to see what is happening. Did some of them guess that the saddest of angel
messengers was passing by?
The clock-hand moves; the angel has passed.
(When this fearful zephyr has howled away,
not a soul is going to be whistling that love-aria from Act
2 —
not even me…I can't remember how it goes).
Wistfully the marble tritons blow their horns, regretfully
Neptune and Mercury linger upon their entablatures.
Sometimes he feels he is cracking up or fading out, and he
avoids the newspaper obituaries because…
How sad that her bonfire that night,
which she saw as a beacon of truest dedication, should
have been interpreted ever since as
a conflagration of betrayal. But what she did, she did
for love.
An ironic gift…to attract and to sadden, both at the
same time.

Even imagined love is true!
An alarmingly androgynous figure of Victory crowned it,
winged and helmeted.
I have always been attracted by the idea of a life of crime.

Coda to Jan Morris

*

p. 59

p. 98 Still there, but derelict

p. 106

> It claimed to honor the dead…but neglected to say
>
> which country they had died for

p. 146 Surgery

p. 148 Perilous brink

p. 159 Invented town

p. 164 Dilapidation

p. 177 Sad ends

> Like a skewed demonstration of old functions

p. 183 Gypsy

p. 184 New activity

p. 185 Best by being itself

p. 187

p. 191 A galvanizing dream

Jan Morris' *The World / Conundrum*

The traffic diverts itself and races away, leaving the poor
lost soul behind.
It seems to be partly physical, partly mental, and partly,
perhaps, too much coffee.
If he sits on a bench, after a moment he gets up again.
If he takes a turn around the grass, he abruptly stops.
Sometimes he looks up at the hill above, but it seems only
to disappoint him,
as if he cannot see what he is looking for up there.

Every new art Deco furniture boutique
is an expression of regret.

[They] have accepted their station in life,
no longer swaggering through the years
with the endearing braggadocio of their tradition, but
more resigned,
more passive, even (perhaps) a little disillusioned.

I hope I made another contribution to the fashioning of
these *objets d'art*.
I hope I gave them, if nothing else, an understanding
of love.

It was my specialty.

Late-Night Confidential

There are certain things that I'll just never do —
I've had to learn to live with that.
I'll never turn to you some evening in a smoky bar,
some late-night confidential with the two of us
commiserating well into the wee hours, smoke
ascending from our cigarettes, the whiskey
hunkered in our voices as I take another drag
and say world-wearily: "Let me tell you
something about women"...

What I can tell you, though, is this: on weekends
at the Little Caesar's in my neighborhood, there is
a woman working in the back, a woman
with a squarish face, blond, rather oddly long
straight hair, her sideburns not quite naturally
not there, a certain something in the limbs,
the trace of something dark above her lips.

And I'm not certain why I tell you this, except
I used to see her sometimes as I stumbled home at 2:00 am
on Saturdays, the bars on Halsted Street just emptying
and I and all the other unpicked gayboys
trying to fill that spot with something stood there
watching, watching as the boyfriends picked up pizzas
for their girlfriends and she worked there

filling orders, one lean, long, depilatoried arm
surrounded by a half-moon silver bracelet
reaching up to spin the order wheel, the silk blouse
molding to her modest breasts. One day,
as I was taking in my shirts,
I saw her walking toward me: high heels,
long tan coat, some little hoopy earrings,
and I almost spoke. You see, I wondered how it was
for her. I wondered how it went those evenings
when she left the Little Caesar's, walked
the Sunday-quiet streets back to her room
and greeted, what? Was anybody there?
Or did she, as I think, walk in and hear the silence,
maybe stroke the cat, and go to bed alone?
I think I have an inkling of the little song and dance
she must have done those evenings
when she did bring someone home, the mild defiance
as she said, "You see, there's something you should know"...
Somehow, I picture her in high school — even then
a woman — dressing in the locker room with an awareness
of her difference, long hair covering her breasts:
a trim and feminine Godiva, nude,
among the rowdy boys in jockstraps.

You see, I know that difference — it is mine
as well: the endless high school years
of dating for appearances, the college girls

I took home early, so I could go out
to the bars, the vague thought troubling me
that they might call me at my dorm; the endless
weddings, baby showers, and incorrect assumptions
one endures. And when one does come out
at last, asserts the right to lead
a "normal" life, the epithets
hurled in the nighttime streets, the stares
in grocery stores, the questions
at the restaurant or hotel; or, just as bad,
the thought that being gay is somehow easier today.
Last week, a woman said to me,
"You couldn't possibly begin to understand
the way it is for women. You're a man."
When I protested I was gay, I knew a little bit
about oppression, too, she paused, then said:
"Well, you can pass, at least. You have that luxury."

I wonder if I'll see the woman in my neighborhood
again, or if I'll have the luxury of "passing"
some night out on Halsted Street, if I should happen on
a band of angry straights. It's true
I don't know what it's like to be a woman, and I'll
never turn
to you some evening in a bar, presuming I can tell you
all about them. But the woman at the Little Caesar's
in my neighborhood — that woman I know just a
bit about.

Psalms

I am a hymnal of my own making.

Spencer Reese

"Vines, Youth"

(Albert Camus, Notebooks)

"Denn alles Fleisch es ist wie Gras" I sang in concert choir
in high school,
lusting over Hayden Harrison, believing not the words nor
in a God
nor that a love could ever be reciprocal — at least, not love
like that,
the sunlight falling on him beautifully in ruby, amber hues,
through stained-glass windows high above the goth-
ic-arched interior
where Hayden stood, the blond hair curled around
his temples,
framing warm brown eyes; his butter yellow sweater bulging at the chest,
and pouched just slightly at his waist, the white shirt
tucked into his jeans,
which crinkled slightly round his beautifully
formed thighs.
At intermission, he played Frisbee in the alley: unselfcon-
scious, gorgeous,
pink disk floating from unblemished hand into the cloudless blue sky,
caught by some elect and chosen other; bright October
sunshine fresh-washed,

dry, illuminating every inch and crevice of the church, the
alleyway —
all things in high relief except my longing, lurking like
the devil
underneath the altarpiece. "There's something so mysteri-
ous about Catholicism,"
said a friend, a fellow Protestant (I now know — relish,
even — that all Protestantism,
literally, is a form of protest). "Yes," I said, still watching
Hayden. "Impressive."
I had not yet embraced the body as a church, had not yet
worshipped at
the shrine of love: I sang my dead songs wracked with guilt
inside an airless tomb.

Ode on a Grecian Urn

The instructor said: "Find every piece of criticism
ever written
on Keats' *Ode on a Grecian Urn.*"

Grad. School, Madison, mid-winter, 1983.
We groaned, even as we (thought we) understood
the lesson:

before you write an article, you have to survey
everything that's come before.
"Beauty is truth; truth, beauty" and all the endless dis-
course over
what that meant.

My classmate and I scoured card catalogs for weeks,
making our entries, working through

each item in the *Bibliography of Reference Sources.* Now,
I can remember very little of it all,
except the very vivid memory of my handsome, blond-
haired partner,
turning to me in the sun one day to say Lord Elgin's name.

He pronounced it with a hard "g."

Magnificat

The sexiest thing
I've ever seen in my life

was a bass
during a performance of an oratorio –

Monteverdi echoing
among the gothic arches of the stone cathedral

as the massed choirs rang;
he stood there, handsome, masculine (he'd

caught my eye before the singing started).
As the orchestra began,

this handsome, black-tuxedoed man
planted his feet the way a bodybuilder does

displaying a "double biceps" pose,
and slowly, slowly sang:

Magnificat, Magnificat,
MAGNIFICAT!

Matthew, Mark, Luke...

Upon my bed by night,
I sought him whom my soul loves;
I sought him, but found him not;
I called him, but he gave no answer.

Song of Solomon

Platonic Love; Moonshine

Sometimes when we were sitting in the late-night dorms,
drunk, in our underwear, our college bodies bare,
the hair appearing so astonishingly on
your upper lip, beneath your arms, and on your chest;
me looking at you with the awe a colt feels toward
a stallion; our mouths close, the scent of you so warm;

collapsing into bed together, waking in
each other's arms — I really wish, one of those nights,
flush with your charms (that mouth, those eyes, Oh, *petite
morts!*);
the way the hair washed down your chest and
thighs, thinned
and disappeared into your sweat-soaked shorts) — I wish
one of those nights I'd blown past caution, past alarms

and every previous abort; reached down to take
you in my mouth; acted decisively, and sucked
the indecision out of you; let loose the impulse
my whole body felt, and which I'm almost certain
rose in yours; unsheathed our swords; dipped oars.
In short, my dear, Oh, how I wish we'd fucked!

But, such was not to be. *O tempora, O mores!*
(I've never felt — before or since — a skin as soft as yours).

Why did we never open up those doors? Cautious,
our galleons hugged their separate shores, left unexplored
that *terra incognito*; our souls bound
together like a single body with two cores —
a heart not wholly mine, nor (dare I say it?) yours.

Campus Paths

Poems are a rubric —
intersection of
Ideas.

Prose is a long walk where a person takes you by the arm,
walks down the hallway with you and descends the creaky,
wooden stairs, opens the strangely heavy, Georgian doors
beneath the dusty, fly- and spider-specked lunettes, ushers
you into the warmly humid June night redolent of faded
tulip trees, the twitter of the birds and languid droning of
the locusts calling to you in the middle of the quad as he
points across the dimming lawns to indicate a low, two-
story, 60s-era red-brick building far off in the distance,
takes his leave of you, and you continue — even more
unsteady now — beguiled by those forest floor brown eyes.

In the oft-told tale about the college campus,
newly built and freshly seeded in the spring,
The President, when asked where sidewalks should
be placed,
replies:
Just let the students walk to classes for a month.
They'll show you where to pave.

What never gets discussed is all the people who,
on countless unmarked paths,
and even with the best-intentioned guides,
get lost.

"There Are Persons Born Without a Sense of Wonder,"

My shrink said, and he, I think, meant you.
Now you're asleep, left somewhere there behind me
and I'm hurtling through the night sky
trying to start anew. Is that Lake Michigan? Its
penile contours
blurred by night or, simply, emptiness?

"What kind of intimacy were you looking for?
You were in love with him?" He asked. (My nod).

"And you kept hoping he'd respond?"

Yes,
Now I see its broad shape forming underneath me
in the dark, and even then, I couldn't see for what it was.
It was too fast, too close. And, are we past it now?

But, there, I see another brightness, hovering at its edge —
a strange, urban aurora that seems menacing at first.

"You have to write your own myth, make a new start.
That's all."

Now the runway is approaching, bright with possibility,
and that phallic tip is gone.
You can't imagine what it's like for me — how hard!
You cannot even dream.

Loneliness

Coming home each evening
to the same depression on the bed
you left that morning.

Monk Parrot

So incongruous and solitary, moving through the grey
skies of Chicago, "Look," she says, "Monk Parrot!"
I look up toward the sky and hear the chattering,
but I have lost him: I have left him there
behind me. "See there, in that tree? A pair
of them escaped ten years ago, and now
they live here in Hyde Park." And why not leave?
Why stay there in that trap? So strange now
to be back — so many years have passed.
"They come from Argentina — even stay here
in the winter." So of course, one can survive, the weather
will be harsh, but I've been through all that before.
Birds migrate. That's the thing — they fly. But I am
leaving him for good — I'm never going back.
What were the first birds moving toward?
How did they know they'd find it? Parrots,
lived here once in Illinois, and they've returned now,
making a new home. "Right there!" Peg says,
and now I see him, swooping through the strange skies
looking for a mate. Oh, yes, Monk Parrot! Squawking
in that green voice, 'Here I am again!'

Poem Written on an Epigraph

Perhaps he did not know yet that the root of all wisdom comes from having loved someone. Evelyn Waugh

Or perhaps he did not know yet

Love is like a tree, its branches filled

with yellow butterflies: as one approaches it,

they float away like dandelion seeds. Bare limbs,

a cold grey wind, a truth

as hard as bark.

The Water Table

Looking at the drifts of snow piled up this morning makes
me think
about the water table. I begin to understand now (once,
though, I did not):
some of the snow will melt, and swell the unseen reser-
voirs; but much of it is lost:
it simply blows away, evaporates, is gone.

In the Bible parable — Old Testament, I think — a man
asks God
to grant a miracle. God tells him: "Lay a wet cloth on
the ground,
and in the morning, you shall find the ground still dry." It
is a metaphor
I still remember: God so powerful he can command the
elements not to combine —
no single molecule of water seeping down into the soil, the
way two bars of gold and silver,
side by side for centuries, will never merge.

It was the way I loved you: mounds of me heaped up
against you
like a snowbank, but no atom of me ever seeping through
—

not one iota all those years. But things combine and
recombine. It's possible
there's even part of me in you, although you never
wanted it.

This frigid morning on my way to work, crossing a bridge,
I see the river, seemingly impossibly not frozen,
wisps of water rising through the air like worms after
a rainstorm,
boundaryless and lost. It is the moisture that's been rising
and transforming
for millennia, the water in the blood of dinosaurs; of me;
of you.

There's an exchange that takes place. It is invisible.
The waters in me swelled for so long, then dried up; I don't
know where
the reservoir stands now. I only know I thought of you
again today.
It's been a million years.

After Image

Traveling to Homecoming at Thornton
after 20 years,

I think back to the first time
I came down to see the college
with my parents:

It was foggy,
and the school was 12 long, agonizing miles
off from the interstate.

We found the college, finally,
and later, in another kind of fog, I met and fell for Kyle,
the straight man I adored for so long, unrequited.

I was coming back now,
with my partner of 11 years — my wonderful and unexpected love —
remembering suddenly the science class experiment we'd
done in 7th grade:

we stared at colored spots for 30 seconds, trying not
to blink.
Then, when we looked at something neutral,
we could see the image still there, burned into our retinas.

For more than ten years I had been in love with Kyle –
a vast and fruitless epoch —
focused hard on (re) creating something
that was really never there.

Cedarburg: Seeing Kyle

Driving unfamiliar from Chicago
north on busy interstate, through
beery, guiltily church-steepled
and incongruously Calatrava-ed old Milwaukee;
past the port with all its boats and rusting tankers
north to Cedarburg,
through summer cornfields
15 rural, outer-Styx miles more to find you
after many years.
My lover of almost a decade by my side,
we turn into the unknown suburb,
cross the train tracks,
take the turn to downtown
with its winery, its vintage woolen mill,
turn accidentally onto your street and then
start screening the facades of white and grey subur-
ban bungalows
until we find your number,
turn into the yard
littered so startlingly with hot wheels, bicycles,
and day-glo orange balls,
a Volvo (I remember
how you always wanted one!)
parked in the open, bicycle-encumbered gloom;
and you, inside the double-car garage,

now stepping out — grey haired —
a toddler in your arms, another
creeping up behind you shyly,
eying us, suspicious,
as you wave us in and reassure us
this is you, your home, your life, your children,
and the woman with whom you now share your life.
Hello my long-lost friend;

goodbye.

A Queer Story

That was the time when all things missed
by just a little: elevated trains,
not fully into stations, disgorged passengers
in air; drunk freshmen,
heading home from bars, inserted keys into
mistaken slots, and I
roulette-balled through the straight streets desperate for
a berth.

Those were the long years when
I passed you every morning on the platform and
you waved
to someone else:
there goes my love, a gesture of farewell
on a departing bus.

Oh, first love!
If I could have opened up
a slightly different portion of
your heart
it would have changed
the world.

A Glimpse

Over the years, I've assembled a little liturgy
of stolen glances – boys

whose rooms I still pay visits to
in fantasies:

Bo Hanson flexing in the high school bathroom,
as we all looked on, amazed;

Jim in his dorm room: tall, athletic
in his underwear; Eric, in

maroon shorts with his blond hair
when he let me feel his biceps. You might think

it is a little sad
to keep revisiting these glimpses of astonishing male
beauty – Yet

each single vision could sustain one
an eternity.

Acts

Then, as if the heads were moved by one muscle, all the faces were turned towards him with wide, derisive grins. He seemed to hear some one make a humorous remark in a low tone. At it the others all crowed and cackled. He was a slang phrase.

Stephen Crane, *The Red Badge of Courage*

New Orleans

It is not the dirty tangle
    of the sheets you leave behind you
        as you walk the pre-dawn streets, the vacant taste
           of last night on your lips. "In New Orleans,
           one does things

one wouldn't do in any other place."
    The early morning mists obscure the deshabille
        of clothes pulled back on from the strange chair
           as you pick your way among the fog-
           bound doorways,

smell of urine here, a flick of interest
    there, the blameless homeless man
        still curled up in his crouch against the cold,
           a shattered bottle rattling inside

a rumpled paper sack.
    It is, in fact, this mounting dawn you would avoid,
        the eerie lack of consequence — its silence
           deafening and awful as your sense of sin
           once seemed.

anonymous sex

meaning: the encounter in the bar,
the wooded glen or alleyway;
the rending of the clothes,
the neediness
and hunger. I don't understand

the way my baby's face
has blurred. anonymous,
I think they mean, because
confronting

the incredible specifics of
this man: the nipples and
the chest, the rippled
abdomen, this vortex of
his thighs,

I don't know who I am.

The Varieties of Religious Experience

One hardly needs examples; but for love, see p. 167, note; for fear, p. 149; for remorse, see Othello *after the murder; for anger, see* Lear *after Cordelia's first speech to him; for resolve, see p 165 (J. Foster case).* -William James' note re CONVERSIONS

How many hot-tar nights
I dragged myself through the cindered streets,
the acrid, warm exhaust of other lovers,
trying to find the one

obscure but certain doorway
that would finally admit
me. How many
drags. How much

despair? For love,
do not see any of the lean years 1 through 30;
for remorse: see all of them.
For anger: see above.

For resolve: look here.

Lamentations

How doth the city sit solitary, that was full of people!
Lamentations, I:1

4 a.m., Near Canada

"Ride the dog!" you howled –
"The dog's the only way to go!"
And popper-high those disco summer nights,
you half-convinced us of the light.
There was a glow, a soft,
mirage-like luminosity that I assumed
derived from towns; but you,
crouched in the Greyhound's feral dark
in sight of Canada, said, "That's the dawn:
we're so much higher now
that we can see the light." Steve,
are you closer to it now? Now that the sun
floats up without you, and I sit,
abruptly sober, through these long
and idling hours?

We could never make that trip again:
the bleary-eyed survey of depot men's rooms,
auto-piloting
through every late-night spot,
the hurried-up connections,
riding on with anybody, anywhere.

These days I don't go out, see anyone:
I sit and read until the light is gone. And then,
I think about that trip, the way
we rooted through the landscape,
hungry for the light.

Audubon in New Orleans

"In the doors of Bourbon Pub,
the beautiful, exotic creatures dance shirtless in the mid-
day sun,
their headdresses resplendent

underneath the rainbow signs.
This morning in the Frenchman's Market, emerald greens
and oranges of Carolina Parakeets in great profusion,

blacks and whites and reds of Ivory Bills* mixed in with
grey Night Herons, all splayed limply, rotting in the
stalls. *Perhaps*
great beauty never can be rendered fully

nor appreciated properly
until it's dead, eh, mon Cherie? Some say
the eggs and feathers I collect — the gorgeous specimens
—

are my attempt to pin down flight. My earliest memory is
un perroquet my mother set free from its cage in care-
free Nantes;
a monkey ripped the bird to shreds.

My work is but a static illustration of the world.
The young men dance in bars.
The yellow fever comes."

Note: many of the species Audubon describes are now extinct - Ed.

Apropos of Nothing

Silence = Death.

What is that sound?
Slightly static, like a radio
come into tune,

but then gone past. Or
a sound that follows you,
down through the centuries, like

"Boyer."

*

Oh, lover,
fragrant with nonoxynol,

just now I saw my life pass by
as at a morgue:

give me a moment to be alone with
my own body.

*

"Of all sexual aberrations,
abstinence is
the strangest."

(Letter
to the Editor
of
Time).

*

The most beautiful objects
at an art gallery
are always
the people in the room.

*

Before you came along,
I was a garden hose,

writhing and spraying out
in all directions,

terrified and lonely as
the day when I first heard of God.

*

(God may, of course, exist,
but I don't put a lot of faith in it.
These days, I sing

a special atheist's mass,
featuring:
Cum Grano Salis, and *Non Credo)*.

*

"The object
is not to die for the revolution,
but to live for it."

(Birds
Without
Wings).

*

Silence = Death.

Listen, can you hear it? As we're talking on the phone,
the ambulance is crossing from my neighborhood
and into yours.

The Drill

This May morning when the air raid siren goes off,
I recall those grade school years
of sitting in the classrooms with the windows open,
dandelions budding on the new-green lawns
and hearing it — the air raid siren — being
tested downtown.

It was time for drill: time now for all of us to hide beneath
our desks, to practice what we'd do if bombs began to fall.
This was Moline, Illinois, late '60s, early '70s,
when fear of war was real enough, the yellow
sirens sounding
every Thursday, 10 a.m. on tall, unpainted poles.

The terror I remember, though, was not of bombs, but
that my mom or dad would find the stack of *Muscle Digests*
underneath my bed, or that they'd notice that
I *didn't* notice girls; fear that someone like Jeff or Bill
would think I liked them — that they'd meet me
after school
and pound me in the bushes. I was not afraid of Russians
dropping bombs, but of my own dropped hints,
my own, untrustworthy proclivities.

Ah, yes, the paranoia of attack.
The siren's done at last.
That man just glanced at me.
See how my eyes cut quickly down?
See how I've learned to duck?

Of Longing in the Mall

I remember standing here in high school in the Walgreen's,
which was then an entrance to the mall, but now is blocked
and locked up somewhere in the middle.

Just as now, the aisles were packed with light bulbs
and extension
cords, and just across from them, a small display
of puzzles,
one of which I desperately wanted, but was afraid to buy –
an image of

a barely clothed Ron Ely as *Doc Savage: Man of Bronze* –
ripped shirt displaying perfect abs, great chest,
and one particularly prominent nipple. I was 17 or
18 then,

and this was 30 years ago. Nobody knew I had this savage
urge. There,
at the fag-end of the 1970s, I couldn't quite imagine walking up to buy it
at the register, let alone assembling it, or showing it
to anyone.

Whatever way I looked at it, my lust was inconve-
nient. Now,

the packages of underwear in stores are more erotic than
that box, and kids today
aren't all that fazed by someone's being gay. So, here
I stand,

a middle-aged man in the middle of a changed mall, con-
juring my lost lust
for a character that isn't even real. And yet, somehow,
I felt compelled to put it all together, finally, for you.

Wish

He told me I was young and hot,
and when he laid his hand upon my back,

there, in that smoky, Madison, mid-winter bar,
I thought I might explode. This was my wish:

to meet a man and have sex for the first time.
In seconds, we were out the door and in his car,

where we began to kiss and clutch like magnets,
both attracted and repelled. His hair was long

and straggly, but his body was as firm and hard
as farm boys' bodies are, and he was earthy:

as we stripped our clothes off,
he began to tongue my crack; then,

when he kissed me later on, it nauseated me. That's
my most vivid memory, that and the fear —

fear he would give me AIDS; fear we were doing wrong;
fear of the frank way he was making love to me.

He drove me later on to meet his friends –
me nervous and uptight the whole time, as I'd been

when he first put my penis in his mouth:
he'd sucked until I couldn't stand it anymore –

that airy suction in a void. It felt immense! But then
it struck me I was having sex now, I was gay now,

I was galavanting off across Wisconsin cornfields with a
total stranger.
Panicked, wanting just to extricate myself,

I told him that I had to go home, feeling awful
as I heard the hurt apparent in his voice. Today,

what bothers me is not how cruel or rash or sleazy I was,
but how guilty and uptight. Thinking of it now, aroused as
I remember

how his tongue explored my body, how my hand clung to
his biceps,
touched his pointed nipple, felt his hard, young, earnest
body on me,

I wish I had stuck my tongue deep in *his* ass.
I wish I'd just relaxed and let myself get blown.

Romans

He that loveth not knoweth not God; for God is love.

First Epistle of John 4:8

Poem for the Lambs

All his life, they've said:
Your inclinations are a sin.
The love you feel is unacceptable.
You'll burn in hell.

Their judgments hound him off a bridge;
toss him from rooftops;
drip slow poison in his veins.
He holds the knifeblade

of their disapproval
hard against his wrists.
He shoves the truth of who he is
into an unlit stove.

Raise up a child in Jesus
and there's nowhere left to go.

Poem for Matthew Shepard

Walking past the flower beds today,
I see a dandelion

lying on the sidewalk,
tossed there by some gardener's hand:

limp blossom, torn leaf cluster, dying root.
Who marks the garden's edge? Who dares to plant that
fence?

Each thing that lives demands we make a place for it.

Gay Bashing

You callous boys
        who swing your bats
in dandelion fields,
        take heed:

for every head you scatter, senseless,
        to the winds,
we shall return
        a thousandfold.

Fragments from an Unidentified Tragedy

oiled youths, in the mid-day sun
wrestling at the gymnasium.

*

His locks were brown,
and the down on his thighs as fine as [

*

(Thus devolves the golden phoenix)

*

Do not confuse the force of love with its object.

*"I'm afraid I'm a broken yardstick in that regard. Everyone
under the age of 25 seems beautiful to me."*

*

[a youth,
beautiful,

*

lost]

Strigil

S-curved implement of bronze
found in the exercise yard at Pompeii —

this verdigris-patinaed tool
that last traced contours of

an olive-oiled athlete's body —
locked inside a glass case in the Field Museum

all these centuries hence:
how vividly you conjure up an image of those boys

I worshipped in the sunshine of
my ineradicable youth.

Judges

A new commandment I give unto you, that you love another; as I have loved you.

John 13:34

Early in the Relationship

This morning in the strangely still (and still-
new) house,

I find the little traces indicating
you are here:

the water droplets
running slowly down the inside of the shower door,

the yellow washcloth
hanging wetly on the smooth white plastic rod,

a few stray whiskers
on the porcelain sink; and in the silvered mirror

somewhere there behind my image,
yours —

this other spirit in the house: wet fog
upon the glass;

used coffee cup left in the kitchen sink,
spoon rattling inside it, signifying: *satisfaction*; *occu-
pancy*; *home.*

*

Armistead Maupin: *Some people think we finally become adults when both our parents have died; for me it happened when someone desired the person I'd become.*

Gaydar

"How do you know?" a friend of mine once asked.

"You know," I said.
"Gay people always know. It's something
in the eyes, I guess — or just that
they look back.

You get real good at looking for
the slightest sign of hope."

Passive (Passage of the Illinois Civil Unions Bill, 6/1/2011)

It's so much easier to be passive
than to stand against the current. Sometimes,
though, there is no other choice except
to be

the stone
that splits the stream.

Revelation

Therefore...bring thy gifts to the altar...Leave there thy gifts before the altar, and go thy way.

Matthew 5:23

Assos

Sunrise on the rocky path beside the sea;
Lesbos in morning mist across the calm blue waters.
Aristotle lived here in this little village for two years,

before he left to tutor Alexander.
Susurrus of waves beneath me on the cliffs,
a goat bell in the hills above.

The same sound then as now.

A momentary peace;
warm smell of dung and wild oregano
wafts up across the mountain.

My partner and I now have been to Istanbul, Gallipoli,
Troy, Pergamon and Ephesus:
wars, religions, myths.

Aristotle, in your birthplace,
lead me in morning darkness like a pedagogue.
I'm here. I have arrived:

Let go.

Latin – The Study of a Sign

a sequence of gestures that, little by little, have lost…all meaning").

iv. He who prays in church should understand what his lips pronounce.

> (we should incline our heads in passing to our monu-
> ments to the dead,

but not make a religion of them)

Thomas Paine – (A Deconstruction) *from* Christopher Hitchens' *Books That Shook the World)*

When Paine made his way back to Europe,

he was one of those slender reeds

that contain the flames stolen so audaciously

from the gods themselves.

"The evolution of theology,

from polytheism to only one God,

is getting nearer and nearer to

the correct figure"...

Epiphany

I desperately want
the manger
to have meaning.

But, to me it's just a barn,
the baby just a baby,
mom and dad
two homeless people.

Maybe that's the problem:
everybody keeps insisting that
they're MORE than people:

Why can't that be enough?

Corpus Christi

The palm fronds bend the way
they have for centuries:

it is time we loved.

What it Looks Like

Looking out
my highrise window
I can see
the man across the distance
bobbing in and out of
sunlight.

At first, I think,
What is he doing?
Then I see
the book, the braids
and realize:
he's rocking
in that Orthodox, Hasidic way.
How curious, that

what I took for
singing, fucking,
was, indeed, a
prayer.

Religion

When I think of all the books I've entered,
kneeling reverently, as if in a temple,
taking in the architecture slowly
as my eyes become accustomed to the light,
the altarpiece becoming more apparent
as I grow aware of all the other congregants beside me
hushed amid the gloom,

I start to understand at last
the impetus behind a Latin mass
whose words are common
to us all.

After

(2013)

For my mother and father,

and for Angie and Jerry O'Hara

You wanted to kill your father in order to be your father yourself. Now you are your father, but a dead father.

Sigmund Freud

The Interior is all ruin.

Shelley.

Contents:

I.

Help

My father and I have a fundamental disagreement about
what "help" is:
he says the only way to help someone is
to do things just exactly the way they want them done;

I'm of the school that help is help:
you let go of the way you want it done, and thank
the person
for the job they did.

I'm visiting my father on the eve of my 49th birthday (he is
84),
trying to assist him with the yard work, but he's prov-
ing fussy,
growing agitated at the slightest change in his routine. I
trim the hedge,

but not in the direction he is used to. He yells at me:
"You do everything too fast! You don't listen! That's why
you got fired!"
I know this is nonsense (I was laid off), but the comment
stings, and

all day long I can't get over feeling small and help-
less. Later,

I go jogging down a blacktopped country road (the smell of tar,
the hum of telephone poles),

thinking back to when I used to ride my bike here summer afternoons,
the lazy trips back from the Y when I was feeling listless,
lonely — even suicidal. Why was that? What could
have caused

those kind of thoughts even back then? Was it a sense
that, someday,
I'd still be here, feeling fatherless, rebuked by
voices overhead?
Could I have had a sense that, someday, I would still be on
this road?

Through the Telescope

It takes a while to locate,
wobbling in and out of sight;

then, as my father reaches out to focus it for me,
I spy Mars hanging terribly above our house.

Poem for a Father

The huge old oak tree
overspreads the ground
so nothing else can grow;
the saplings fade and
die:

someday the grass will be your legacy.

Poem for a Mother

On a chilly beach, the green sea turtle
lays her eggs

and never, ever,
looks on them again.

Twenty Days of Falling

In Hesiod, Time (Kronos)
eats his children

to prevent them from succeeding
him. The heavens

are the space a hammer falls for 10 days
from the clouds;

the underworld — likewise —
the space a hammer falls for 10 days from the earth.

In toto, then,
the universe is 20 days of falling. All day long

the pine cone weights upon my father's cuckoo clock
have lowered steadily. At 10:00, I pull them up

and once more they begin their slow descent.
Why keep on trying? Why not let the damn thing stall?

God, I wish I believed in
anything at all.

White Java Chicks

White Java Chicks — long thought extinct —
were suddenly and unexpectedly produced,
in a Museum of Science & Industry poultry display,
by accidental combinations of recessive genes.

Near the end of her life in the convalescent home,
my mother tells me, confidentially:
"Your father and I loved each other once,
but it's like a distant memory now."

How am I here?
I seem to have sprung into this world
out of nothing.

How Things Reproduce

Love is
a verb: it festers

like a grain of pollen
in the silky filaments.

It ripens
into fruit

by way of
irritation.

Not a Very Good Day

On the last afternoon of my mother's life,
I am driving across the Illinois prairie to visit
from Chicago.
I phone her in the nursing home
where she lies recovering from a broken hip and,
above the car's roar, I can barely hear her say,
"No, it's not been a very good day –
Not a good day at all."

The sun is slanting spectacularly
on the late afternoon cornfields,
and on the radio, Katy Perry is singing:
"Can you hear my heart racing
in my skin-tight jeans?
Be my teenage dream tonight."

The Great Migration

4:44 p.m.:
An eerie stillness in the patient's room.
Then, suddenly, much activity.

*

One year later,
on the anniversary of my mother's death,
I am in Kenya waiting — hoping —
for a sign, to make sense of it all.

The herds of wildebeest and zebra file past me
in an endless, snaky tumult
trailing down into the valley.
In the distance, Tanzania.
The light grows luminous and strong;
I watch until
it disappears.

That's when I realize —
and, for a moment, understand —
that all of us
are on
the same great journey.

Hand-Me-Downs

There are phrases out there, waiting to be grown into
like hand-me-down clothes —
phrases like: When I went away to college;
When I got my first job, or
When my mother (or father) passed away.

They chafe and irritate at first,
they pull and bind you weirdly. Then,
at last, they fit.

*

The first really expensive sweater I ever bought was
a cowl neck, oatmeal and grey houndstooth at Younker's,
in Moline's Southpark Mall.

I was nervous about buying it (it was expensive),
but my mom said: "Oh, I think it's a really classic weave –
you'll be able to wear that for a very long time."

*

Today, some 30 years later. I am at the same store,
buying a pair of black pants for her funeral, wondering
what somebody will dress me in

the day I die.

Poem for the Morning of a Funeral

For Donna Boyer, 1926 - 2011

A mother
leads
her ducklings
gingerly
out on the morning water,
ripples
widening
to meet
the rising sun:

Where is *my* mom?

Pink Sentinel

When you pick out the clothes you will bury your mother
in, be sure
that's the image of her you want in your mind's eye forever:
her lying in a casket inside a cement vault in her pink suit
with the white lace blouse,

the Mackintosh brooch you bought her in Scotland on
her lapel,
on her fingers the peridot ring from Hawaii. Make sure
that's the way you want to see her
as you think of her lying there in the cemetery in the Open
Bible section,

dutifully facing east awaiting resurrection, because that's
the way you're going to see her
forever and always afterwards, patiently lying beneath the
6 feet of soil
with the same restful expression she had when you bent to
kiss her for the last time.

When you kiss your mother for the last time, make sure
you're ready for
the coldness of her forehead against your lips, or the cool
touch of her hand, somewhat

like chicken wrapped in cellophane. Make sure you're
ready to remember that because

you're going to think of it each time you pull a package
from the freezer at the grocery store —
at least a little while. Make sure you're ready, as you see the
coffin nailed shut for the last time, that you don't watch as
they drive the pegs in,

sealing up the coffin, or you'll think about it each time you
look back upon the funeral —
that moment when they sealed your mom away. Make sure
you're ready for
the casket's unexpected weight as you join all the other
relatives to lift the coffin

from its walnut stand and transfer it into the awful and
ungainly hearse
for its journey to the cemetery, bleak and naked in the
middle of the cornfields.
Make sure that you can bear that weight, because your
mother lies there, all the while,

and waits.

A Day at the Museum

One of the loveliest days I ever remember spending with
my mother was a day at the Museum of Contemporary
Art in Chicago. The day was gorgeous: early May, the apple
trees in blossom. The museum was a glass and steel building overlooking Lake Michigan, which was a robin's egg
blue that day. It was just me and my mom, and I was enjoy-
ing this a-typical time alone with her: usually, my family
went shopping when my parents came to town; this time
we decided to let my dad and sister go off on their own.
My mom had been a "Picture Lady" in my grade school
years – one of a group of PTA mothers who signed up to
bring in posters of master paintings to the classrooms.
Once a month, she'd go to the local library, research the
work, check out the poster, then come to our class to make
a presentation. My mom loved it, and continued doing it
for years, even after I'd completed Junior High and High
School. She had never gotten past her freshman year in
college, and I think she liked the chance to keep up with
her education. Still, I had forgotten that she'd done it,
until — entering the gallery that day — she spied a piece
across the room and said, "Isn't that a Mondrian?" I was
very proud and impressed, and somehow an impression
of my mother came together then of someone who had
never really reached her true potential — one who'd never
had a chance to shine. That day at the MCA, my mom was

wearing a white jacket with large, burgundy roses on it, and her hair was a beautiful snowy white. It's the jacket she's wearing in my favorite photograph of her. She died six months ago, and now I often think about that day, about the fact that afternoon just happened once. The exhibit we took in that day was a retrospective of the artist Chuck Close: gigantic faces all composed via the artist's inky thumbprints. They're the kind of paintings that can only be appreciated from a distance. Up close, they dissolve into a mass of lines and dots that make no sense at all.

Poem for my Mother

Maybe only women have
enough room in them
for another person; my father

never did. The remnant of the sea
all women carry deep inside them
(and in which my mother carried me)

did not drown me. Rather,
it's as though I'm coming up for air

at last,
upon a distant shore.

Troy

(For Bill Boyer)

"In running three times around the city Hector and Achilles thus covered fifteen kilometers." Heinrich Schliemann, *Ithaque, le Peleponnese et Troie*

Just 53 streets describe Moline: they start down at the river (First Street, Second Street, and so on), and run east to 53rd, the street where I grew up. Just at the bottom of the hill is East Moline, a very different world.

*

This narrow path outside the ruined walls of Troy — this alley — is the place where Hector ran around the city three times before he was, at last, defeated.

*

In the alleyway outside my father's house in Moline, snow is falling and the ice upon the ground is thick. My 83-year-old father breaks down, saying, "I can't survive another winter in this house alone."

Thus does another kingdom fall.

Barbarians at the Gate

Socrates said that no one should presume to read
the universe
until he has first read and mastered his own soul.

As the Spartans were at the gates of the city of Athens,
he was still trying to define the nature of fortitude.

My sister called me on Sunday morning to tell me
my father had blood in his urine.

Picturesque French Village

My father loves to tell the story of the trip
he and my mother took as newlyweds:
June, 1950, he and his new bride
driving dusty gravel roads up in the northern
woods of Michigan and Canada; how one day,
seeing on the map the small pink designation
"Picturesque French Village," they'd decided on
a detour of some half a day, the roads of farmland
Canada downgrading first to asphalt, then to gravel,
then to just a sort of muddy rock, until at last
they'd stopped beside a caved-in barn,
grape-strangled by the dusty road,
to ask a man along the roadway
if he knew how far the village was.
"How far?" the man replied, perplexed. "You're *in* it."
Looking 'round amazed, my parents saw
just one imploded barn, a broken pump,
and maybe here or there some vestiges of
walls, but that was all there was.
Down through the years, I've heard him tell this story
half a dozen times at least, to friends or relatives,
but always with such glee, such absolute delight,
you know that he's not sorry. Quite the opposite:
it's one of his most precious souvenirs.

What things can I salvage, what gems
can I rescue from the wreckage, as I saw my father
picking through the rubble of the Paradise Theatre
when I was young?

The Paradise was where my father had his first job
back when he was dating mom. These days,
the space is just a large green rectangle
between two low-rise buildings, one
a J.C. Penney store abandoned in the early 60s,
the other a conglomeration of a few boutiques,
a stamp and coin store, and an army-surplus shop.
In better days, the lot might have been built upon
or been converted to a parking lot,
but with the loss of businesses out to the malls
back in the early '70s, it was decided that
the area would be converted to a mall,
and where the Paradise had stood would be "green space."
Of course, the blocked-off streets and concrete benches
only made the situation worse: the business
wasn't coming back, the gaping hole
between the two low-rises just looked silly.
In my father's day, however, Moline's downtown
was a thriving marketplace with three fine jewelers,
half a dozen clothing stores, a Jupiter
and Woolworth store, a good-sized J.C. Penney's,
Temple's Sporting Goods, The New York Store,

a family candy store called Lagomarcino's,
which is still there, still the way it looked in 1945,
an elegant, late l9th century edifice that held
the local Y, which sat beside a rather squat,
Art Deco post office, and next to that a fine library
in the Greek Revival style.

        And, in the center of all that
there stood The Paradise, a movie house
somewhere between the grand old movie palaces
of larger cities and the thrown-up multiplexes
current now. It was a single screen,
a little balcony in back, but here and there
you saw the touches they would never add today:
the plaster gilt around the doors and ceilings,
frilly cast-iron grilles around the ticket window,
on the doors, and in the air vents; frosted glass
Art Deco lights that threw a long, thin shaft of light
up columns to a barrel-vaulted ceiling where your eyes
could just make out a mural of some kind. That painting
must have been the most impressive thing of all
back in its heyday. Now you only saw it in the movie's
daylight scenes, but even so, the ceiling was amazing:
two huge cloud banks floated on a field of azure,
one off to the left and one more to the right. And on
these clouds cavorted cherubs, minotaurs, pipe-
playing fauns. A team of horses pulled the sun across

the sky, and satyrs mixed with maidens bathing
at the edge of large, still pools.

Of course,
The Paradise had faded by the time that I was little:
age had robbed the ceiling of its color; paint
had flecked off here and there, and there was one large
water spot out in the center of the sky. The red plush
seats had long ago lost all their springs, and sat there
flat, denuded and defeated. Lights were never brought up
in the theater itself, and everybody said
it was because the place would look so bad. The Paradise
was showing late-run movies at this point for 50¢,
but even so, nobody I knew ever went except my family,
and that because my dad had worked there, met my
mother there.
The kids at school said rats would nibble at your toes
unless you kept your feet up on the seats.

One of the last times
I remember going to The Paradise, which was about
the last time our whole family was together, Lynn,
my older sister, was about to leave for college; Larry
in a few years would be entering the National Guard,
and I was just about to enter Junior High. We sat there
watching *Fiddler on the Roof* long after everybody else
had seen it, and, because my sister soon was leaving,

I remember crying at the scene set at the railroad station
when the daughter sings, *Far From the Home I Love*
because she's following her husband to Siberia.
The film broke twice while we were there, and I recall
my father fidgeting, as if he might go straight up
to the booth and fix the thing himself. In fact,
the owner of the theater was still alive, still there,
Abe Brotman, probably the first Jew I had ever met,
and one of just a handful in the area. He'd smile
and shake my dad's hand warmly every time we went,
and though he always asked how things were,
  he was so deaf, he couldn't hear dad's responses.

After that time we were hardly ever all together
as a family again: my sister moved up to Chicago,
I went off to college finally, and didn't think about
The Paradise again.

                    My senior year, on break,
however, Dad said they were going to tear it down
and he was going for a last look. I can't forget
the way he looked as we stood watching
and the wrecking ball tore deeply in the building's side,
exposing to the light of day the prancing minotaurs,
cavorting cherubs, and the half-clad maidens
shrinking from the light; or how, a few days later,
he stood picking through the rubble for a piece of screen,

a bit of painting — anything to keep the dream alive,
the way I watched the shattered theater my father was,
and searched for some way to remember him. Freud says
the most important day for any young man is
the day his father dies, but it is not what I expected.
Now the sunlight's streaming through the slatted
metal blinds
upon my father's suddenly abandoned walls, and I
can hear
a small voice asking me bewilderedly, "How Far? "How
far?
And answering me even more astonishingly,
"This is it. You're *in* it."

Schizophrenic Poem

When my dad died, I felt sorrow and relief.
Dazed, I was sad in the belief that

never more would there be joy.
But, part of me was — dare I say it? —

glad to be done, even (not to be coy)
excited at this new phase, though,
I grant you, that sounds wrong.

My father is dead, my father is dead,
echoed relentlessly inside my head.

Sometimes it felt like a tragedy;
sometimes it felt like a song.

Agamemnon

They told me I had no choice, but really, I did:

"If you want to reach Troy,
You have to sacrifice your child."

When you go to the Oracle,
which is more important:
the answer, or,
the question?

Why My Father and I Never Played Catch

You have to care about the endpoint
of the arc;

the thing that's left your hand —
the thing you've tossed away.

The Mysteries of Greece

When Oedipus kills his father on the road to Delphi,
violence is such a part of that culture,
he doesn't even remember the episode, especially.

Actually, I think,
I didn't kill my father: he killed me.

*

Standing alone on the deck in Paros as the sun sets,
I suddenly realize:
When I was at the Oracle myself,

I never asked a thing...

A Foreign Language

When I was in college, I studied French for two years,
but I was never comfortable with it: I could
never remember
when you were supposed to pronounce the final letters of
words.

For instance, if a word ends in a consonant, you don't pronounce it,
but if it's followed by a vowel, you do. Thus, "sette" is pronounced "set,"
But "set" is generally pronounced like "say."

Often, when I wasn't sure, I'd kind of half-way say them.
In spoken French, too, you can sometimes hear the
ghost of
final consonants appended to the next word.

Now that most of my friends have lost at least one of
their parents
(and I have, too), I can never remember whose mother or
father is still alive,
and whose is not. Thus, when it comes time to ask
about them,

I just kind of elide all mention, much the way my tongue
used to hesitate
when I was speaking French and it came time to decide
whether to articulate those final sounds.

Fathers and Sons

My father could go on and on for hours about anything,
never taking a breath, from time to time interjecting,
"Long story short" but, nevertheless, continuing to
describe, in minute detail, eminently practical things
about which I — and most people, for that matter — had
very little or no interest.

Consequently, I'm a poet.

The Memorial Walk

There's a jogging path in Moline,
beside the river's edge. It's lined with

copper plaques — memorials to loved ones:
the Ydeens (town merchants), Bjustroms (members of

our church), the Skoglunds (neighbors).
It's a pretty walk, and — Oh, my god, Wayne Dull died?

When was that? — it makes it like a small town,
with the cemetery nearby.

You can run through all the dead,
but it's not really necessary:

all the dead are buried
inside me.

Western Illinois Electric

One of my dad's earliest jobs was with Western Electric in the 'fifties,
and, as he talks about it now, it sounds like adventures in a mini sex trade.
There were, apparently, groups of men who had women stashed here and there
in various cities, and the various phone operators and electricians would travel
city-to-city and hook up with each other in places like Albert Lea, Minnesota,
or the Plantation in Moline. My dad got caught up in it several times himself,
seemingly, when he found himself with out-of-town salesmen who corralled him
into visiting brothels in these cities. Of course, he never told these stories
when my mom was alive; now that she's passed away, we regularly hear
stories that go just a little further down the road each time. I'm not sure
why my dad is so preoccupied with telling all this now except, perhaps, that
for the past six decades, they have had no place to go – no outlet –
and so now are flooding down the pathways waiting to be told.

My father's whole life was cut off
in such a way: he left his boyhood home of Iron Mountain
at the age of 13,
and he never quite recovered: all his life was spent in an
attempt to re-capture
some of what he'd lost in moving from there to Moline at
such an early age:
an innocence perhaps lost, an idyllic way of life he never
quite attained again.
My father met my mother, lived here in Moline his whole
life, had us kids,
and never seemed to find the life he wanted. Closest was
his job as a projectionist
at The Paradise Theater, a movie palace of the old sort.
Recently, I went downtown
to see the site where the Paradise had once stood, and all
that's left now is a surreal,
rectangular gash between two other buildings. And yet,
this was the space where
my dad spent his teenage years, lived out his fantasies,
seemed happiest – a place of dreams
which is now merely a gap between two buildings with no
connection to anything at all.

The Bookmobile

In the midst of closing up my parents' house in Moline,
I decide to take a jog around the streets where I grew up.
I start by loping down the sidewalk,
past the towering maple tree I planted as a stick
in grade school, out onto the tree-lined avenue
up to the corner.

Once there, it is a choice of heading past
the houses of my childhood friends,
Steve Cappaert, Jerry Miller, or down the quiet street
up to the top of the hill – same way I walked
in grade school on my way to Cub Scouts. It seemed
far then,
but now takes merely minutes
there and back again.

Once back, I then continue jogging past Ben Franklin
grade school,
looping round the blacktop and the baseball field,
continuing past the tavern at 12th avenue,
then straight ahead to reach my junior high.

Here are the tennis courts I spent so many summer days
upon.

Jogging still, I loop these, thinking of those listless afternoons,
and round the school onto the broad, huge football field
out back,
the small slope where I lost my glasses in the snow one day,
and where — each year — we tried (and failed) our
Presidential Fitness Tests.
I gloat about this now: at 50, I've been jogging for
eight years.
Who would have dreamed that I'd return one day, reclaim-
ing all this turf?

I pass the wing which holds the auditorium,
and think back to the plays I loved to be a part of;
thinking, too, about my dad, and how he tried
to recreate the memories of his boyhood home.
He was desperate not to see the details of his life
get lost – grew frantic trying to impart them all
to me those last days.

As I round the bend and come back home,
I see the spot where mom fell in the yard
and broke her hip; the peonies are trampled still.
Upset, I run on past the house, remembering suddenly
the visits mom and I would always make together
to the bookmobile.

I loved the bookmobile! It came
each Tuesday, and I'd ride my bike a few short streets
away to where it parked beneath a huge old elm,
the coffee smell and hum of it as I walked in each week
and chose a new world with each book: what would it be
this time?
A mystery? A novel? It was endless possibility.

Now, as I run along the street the Bookmobile was
always on,
I see the shady spot is still there, though a house has
sprung up
in the former empty lot. Though I won't be coming to
Moline again,
I think of asking someone if the bookmobile still
stops there,
wondering if they'd have a clue what I was asking them
about. Yet,
as I jog across the spot where, every week
that lumbering, wonderful, improbable, vehicle would sit,
it hits me that the library, now, is me.

Buddhism

The eternal is in the going, the Buddhists say,
meaning nothing
is ever lost. I've been increasingly

more interested in Buddhist thought
since my mother's death — aware of how
my mom is all around me,

like the cloud of dust
from the erasers
I clapped in the atrium at school one day —

the atrium between my second-grade class
and the library.
That was the year I really took up reading,

seizing every book
I could, and mother always there beside me,
teaching me, the sense of her

enveloping me, omnipresent. She was there
in back of everything:
on days I walked the three blocks home for lunch,

the sidewalks wet with puddles,
still, cool, black
beneath the June-green maple trees,

the water full of lucid stones,
the languid ends of worms,
a nacre cloud of mud that swirled and settled,

finally, on the bottom. Mom was in that water.
Mom was in the mud. Mom was the aperture
that opened to the sky.

Cold

In high school,
a friend and I used to engage in a playful game of
one-upmanship:

"Man, it's cold," we'd say. How cold?
"Colder than a witch's tit."
Then, we'd keep on adding things, such as:

"Colder than a witch's tit…
"In a brass bra…"
"Filled with Freon…"

"At midnight…"
"On a cloudless night…"
"At the north pole…"

"On December 31st…"
"Standing naked…"
"After just getting out of a wet bath…"

Looking back,
I realize that — creative as it was —
it was a bit one-dimensional. So now,

based on a few more years' experience, I'd add:

"No job."

"No lover."

"And both your parents dead."

On Removing my Mother and Father's Door Key from my Ring *(12/23/2019)*

What is blooming at that old house
I will never visit anymore?

All those flowers and plants my parents gathered lovingly
from friends of relatives:
the irises and pussy willows, lemon lilies,
peonies;

new owners ripped them out – even the hedge.
Now, the yard feels

boundaryless

The Walnut Room *(Remembrance of Things Past)*

"I am the only one who ever lived who remembers / my mother's voice in the particular shadow / cast by the sky-filled Roman archway" writes Jorie Graham in her beautiful poem *Cagnes-Sur-Mer 1950*; and, as I sit here in the Walnut Room of Marshall Field's department store in Chicago, 2020, watching sunlight filter through the double-story windows on the floral carpet (cream and burgundy), the walnut wainscoting, and beaded crystal chandeliers, I'm thinking

something similar. The elegant Reliance Insurance building (one of the world's first skyscrapers) is to my right, the view straight out of 1893. You get a similar effect by standing near the Wrigley building, looking east towards Tribune Tower and the Intercontinental hotel: it's like you were transported back in time, since your entire field of vision is filled with buildings built in 1929. Just as I'm reminded of the poem,

I can hear Yehudi Menuhin begin to play Bach's *Violin Sonata in A Major* — the exact same record that I listened to incessantly when I first moved here to Chicago, living in my little one room studio on Cambridge street (a building also from the early 1920s), with its parquet floors, its tall, old windows and the French door opening up into the topmost branches of an old elm, which I loved to watch the seasons pass through.

I would sit so often in that studio and listen to the music as the sunlight streamed across my floor, the windows shut, the air conditioner humming in the summer; or, I'd watch the sunlight, weak and grey in winter, as the cold winds howled outside. I loved that studio. It was my first space, my first home here in the city, and I still look up towards the window as I pass there, wondering

who lives there now? I still remember how I had my furniture: the tan plaid sleeper sofa in the center of the room, the stereo against the far wall, and the framed Monet print up above the light oak bookcase. In the corner by the long, tall windows was a palm tree that luxuriated in the light. I spent 5 years in that room, and now no trace of me remains.

The Walnut Room is owned by Macy's now. Fields, as an entity, exists no more.

Memory

Driving past
the house where I once lived —
the porchlight
still burns bright.

II.

Pelagic

Scot's father's ashes sit in a metallic silver urn upon his sister's mantle.

No one knows quite where

to put them.

Notes Upon a Widow's Grief

For Angie O'Hara

She cries a little when she tells the tall, sweaty, tube-socked
man from the lawn service, "My husband's passed away,"
and gives the man the $50 her husband left in an envelope
on their dresser.

She asks you if you want her husband's white work shirts,
still in cellophane.

She points to the batteries she purchased for her husband's
hearing aid, and says:
"What a waste."

*

Midweek, she picks out flowers for the funeral service, and
edits the obituary.

She answers a telephone solicitor and tells them again that
her husband is deceased.

She turns around and speaks to you about him in the pres-
ent tense.

*

She sleeps, for the rest of her days, alone.

Visiting Merritt Island Six Months After My Mother-in-Law's Funeral

Like a bower bird preparing a nest for his mate,
the cute young father scoops up lime green plastic buckets full
of sand
and brings them sloshing up the beachfront
to his blond, pink-suited daughter — two or so — to make
her castle
just a foot or two away from foaming surf.
He does this time and time again. When I look out later,
he's sitting in the center of a huge, round fort with walls six
inches high.
That afternoon, the waves begin to wash it all away.

That evening, as I sit out on my balcony again, I watch a family
set their automatic camera on a bench to take a photograph.
The camera pulses amber several times, until the flash
reveals them
lit against the night. Laughing, they set the camera up
again and,
as the camera flashes this time, they jump into the air. They
keep on doing this,
the point no longer the photograph, but just the act: a leap,
a flash,
and for a moment: happiness.

In Memoriam

for Jerry O'Hara

In the video,
Scot's father sits in the timeshare condo
on vacation, videotaping

the red orb gently emerging from the sea.
"This is Sunrise on the Atlantic Ocean,
May 10, 1985," he says, almost reverently.

Who would have expected such a quiet,
lyrical moment
from such a scrappy, outwardly hard-boiled man?

I think of this on the third anniversary of his death
as I watch the sun come up
without him:

This is Sunrise on Lake Michigan,
March 12, 2010.

The Cries

All these years I've lived here in Chicago,
I've heard that sound over my head,
and never quite known what it was:
a kind of rhythmic, screechy, whining cry
which I assumed was birds or seagulls.

Now, however, standing underneath a building ledge and
hearing it once more, I suddenly associate it with nature
films I've seen where
mother birds return to feed their clamoring, denuded
young, beaks gaping as
the fledglings strain and yearn for morsels from their parents' mouths.

Dear lord, these long years I have struggled in this city on
my own,
examining the bonds with my own family – all these years
I've wandered through the city streets, not realizing
It's the sound of children screaming for their parents
from the gutters.

On the Dock

On this Father's Day, the five-year anniversary of Scot's
mother's death,
(his father gone eight years,
my mother and my father gone now, too),
we gather to "release" their ashes
(Interesting choice of words your niece has made).
Elvis is singing (your mom's favorite);
the skies are blue, the waterway and park your parents' loved
seems like the perfect spot.

An egret plays among the shadows;
light breeze on the water.
Beautiful:
a place between the river and the ocean,
estuary to
the grey Atlantic.

I had thought that what we'd find was closure on your
parents –
possibly an end to sibling squabbles.
But, alas, the ruse does not work: siblings do not show. Yet,
those who loved your parents gather anyway

to tell their stories, share their laughter, say, not so much,
"Farewell," as:
"Thank you. Thank you for all the years you shared,
for giving me your son,
for all the life and love." I am surprised

you pour your parents into one stream
as you release their ashes.
I would not have thought of that, but
it's appropriate: both of them commingled as they were
in life.

The ashes mix; the bits of bone and grit begin to sink.
A greenish patch begins to swirl and moves beneath
the dock,
then out to sea:

Goodbye, beloved in-laws; farewell, parents.
What we're letting go is not the two of them,
but our idea of family.

III.

On the Ocean

Blue-green waters of the bay.
White sails of boats that gently
turn:

late summer moving into autumn.

Poem at 50

The little oval leaf
flaps
in the corner of my windshield

like the reel-change marker in a movie,
flashing once for warning,
then again:

it's time to change. Change now.

Poem in the Workplace

After wracking my brain
while staring at the VDT screen's
blinking cyan cursor; faxing,

answering phone calls with their LED display,
I take a different tack and try to think about it idly,
still recalling in my mind's eye

college: all the warm-hued memories of the library
in winter,
afternoons spent hopefully in research;
writing, making friends and tackling *Moby Dick*,

which reference made me think back to those days
and try to put my finger on the right term in the first place;
decades down the road and sitting

in my starched white shirt
behind the monitor of someone else's writing
at my putty-colored desk

lit with the blue fluorescent glare,
I hit upon the word I've struggled to recall all day:
concordance.

Monday Morning, On the Way to Work

This rain reminds me of the rain that used to fall so softly
on the campus in September,
on the wet, potato skin cement beneath the trees whose
leaves were drying,
changing in the first cool breath of autumn. I would stand
in silence underneath the trees,
the campus still, devoid of life due to the rain, just me and
me alone to hear
the random droplets falling (I could hear them clearly in
their indirection,
each one falling separate and distinct); the light rain
glozening the blacktop;
red brick buildings ringed around me with their promise
and that sense —
that lovely sense — I had of being nineteen and my whole
life opening before me,
tangible, intense.

How easy it was, once, to look into my heart.

Laid Off

Stunned,
with all my pictures,
files, an extra set of shoes,
some desk supplies,
a plant, and who knows what all
shoved into two shopping bags,
I stand there at the strangely empty bus stop,

Waiting.

Intent

Flattened
like a rose
inside the pages of
a fat book,

desiccated.

Memorial Day

Lying in the soft light of my bedroom
on this calm, May afternoon,

I watch the gold light growing clearer, darker,
heavier, like shadows in the deepest part

of ice. Up in the black-xed Hancock building,
lights wink on and off like fireflies, and I imagine

hands that reach
to turn them on or off. I look down at my own,

immobile in the dark.
I think I should turn on a light,

but don't.

Moving Thought

How many more Falls will I move these sweaters
from one closet to another?

The planet tilts and it is Winter; tilts again
and it is hot.

How many more Falls have I got?

Sphere of Influence

Nightly, underneath a silent, blue-black heaven,
the drunk bard
sits atop a corrugated, rain-filled tractor tire
pulled to the middle of a weedy vacant lot
and tosses out his empty, brown-bag-swaddled bottles
in a lazy semi-circle pattern
in the dark.

IV.

The Dilemma

The avocado stillness of the park lagoon;
the June-green light of dusk.
There, in the glassy placidness, I am the only witness as
a goldfish looms up soundlessly,
an instant, gone.

How shall I speak of this without betraying it?

The Amphorae

All my life, I've struggled with the craft
of poetry, obsessing over words and line-
breaks, striving to create the perfect vessel
to deliver what I meant.

*

At the bottom of the sea,
the divers find a Roman shipwreck.
Time has stripped away the wood,
and what remains, still
clustered in a heap
upon the driftless ocean floor?

The amphorae.

Cremona Viola (1619)

Four-hundred-two-year-old viola,
at the concert,
you still sing in honeyed tones.

The sound remains
the same,
the instrument remains

the same. Only the centuries
and ears
have changed.

The Unspoken Poem

For the memorial of your friend,
I think for days about the words or stories
that would best evoke him.
I even memorize a poem
I know he loved. Yet,

when the moment comes,
a toast is raised,
and not a word is spoken,

save his name.

Anniversary

27 years
link-armed with Scot
beside the fire.

As years
go up the chimney,
warming us,

Nina Simone
implores:
Don't leave me.

"Where are the beautiful gay love poems?"

I once wrote
more from despair
than from experience.

And yet,
these poems have been
my life.

"One meets one's fate
on the very road one uses
in order to avoid it."

It is the same road:
my life, these poems,
my love –

Home

It took my parents' deaths for me to call Chicago home,
and even then, I wasn't comfortable.

Columbus, look around:
The cargoholds of grief you launched across the sea

were long ago unloaded. A life has happened –
your life. It is just beginning. It is always

just beginning. See how the waves break
on the shoreline, roiling,

opaque one moment, then, at last,
transparent.

Notes:

Jan Morris and the Meaning of Nowhere is a found poem, based entirely upon the rearranged text of Jan Morris' memoir, *Trieste and the Meaning of Nowhere*. The poem appeared in the *Windy City Times*, 6/20/2007.

Vines, Youth: "Denn alles Fleisch es ist wie Gras" is a line from Brahms' *German Requiem*.

Platonic Love; Moonshine takes its title from a line in Constance Garnett's translation of Tolstoy's *War & Peace*.

Reading The Young Eagle: The Rise of Abraham Lincoln is another found poem, based in part upon the text of Kenneth J. Winkle's book of the same name.

Fragments from an Unidentified Tragedy: the quote is Plato quoting Socrates.

Footnote King James is based upon several annotations in the *Revised Standard Version* of the Bible, published by Oxford University Press.

Latin, the Study of a Sign is a poem extracted from the text of a book with the same name by Francoise Waquet.

The Origin of Consciousness in the Breakdown takes it's title from Julian Jaynes' *The Origin of Consciousness in the Breakdown of the Bicameral Mind*. "Tribeless, lawless, hearthless one" is a quotation from Aritsotle's *Politics*. "He had fallen in love with the past, a profitless love" is a line from Thomas Flanagan's *The Tenants of Time*.

Columbus in the New World - Acknowledgments

I would like to acknowledge the publications in which the following poems previously appeared, some in slightly different versions: "Looking at the Moon Inside the Aerospace Museum," and "On Staring Too Long at the Sun," in *Gents, Bad Boys and Barbarians: New Gay Male Poets*; "Columbus in the Plague Years" in *The James White Review*; "Homer Loses the Thread" and "I am the Apple of my Father's 'I'" in *708*; "My Father Meets My Lover" (which first appeared as "On a Mountaintop in Early Autumn"), in *The Dallas Review*; "New Orleans" in *The Queer Planet Review*; "Weeds" in *The Evergreen Chronicles*; "Late Night Confidential" in *The Pittsburgh Quarterly*; "Linnaeus at the End," and "Archaeology" in *Art Word Quarterly*; "The Man in Walgreen's," "Monologue Inside a Bar," and "A Sunday in the Early Fall" in *Red River Review*; "Columbus in the New World," "Winter, Chicago, 1985," and "Tarzan as a Gay Man" in *King Log*; "Stonewall 25" in *The Windy City Times*; "The Disease," *Chiron Review*; "Jan Morris and the Meaning of Nowhere," *Windy City Times*; "4 a.m. Near Canada," *The Gay Review (Canada)*.

Thanks

I would like to thank the following people for help with these poems over the years: Leslie Ullman, Mark Cox, Mark Doty, Michael Moore, David Feela, and Cassie Mainiero. Last, but certainly not least, I would like to thank Scot O'Hara for a lifetime of love and support. Without him, I'd never have been able to find a true new world: happiness.

Dale Boyer is the author of a novel (*The Dandelion Cloud*), a short story collection (*Thornton Stories*), and a children's book (*Justin and the Magic Stone*, with artwork by Dan Holder). He attended Blackburn College (B.A.), The University of Wisconsin-Madison (M.A), and Vermont College (M.F.A). His reviews have appeared regularly for many years in *The Gay & Lesbian Review Worldwide*. He is originally from Moline, Illinois, but currently lives in Chicago with his husband, Scot O'Hara. Visit him at **www. DaleBoyerWorks.com.**